PRESENTING
S. E. Hinton

TUSAS 528

Twayne's United States Authors Series
Young Adult Authors

General Editor: Patricia J. Campbell

The Young Adult Authors books seek to
meet the need for critical studies of fiction
for young adults. Each volume examines
the life and work of one author, helping
both teachers and readers of young adult
literature to understand better the writers
they have read with such pleasure
and fascination.

PRESENTING
S. E. Hinton

Jay Daly

Twayne Publishers • Boston
A Division of G. K. Hall & Co.

Copyright 1987 by Jay Daly.
All rights reserved.
Published by Twayne Publishers
A Division of G. K. Hall & Co.
70 Lincoln Street
Boston, Massachusetts 02111

First printing

Copyediting supervised by Lewis DeSimone
Book design by Marne Sultz
Book production by Janet Zietowski

Typeset in 10/13 Century Schoolbook
by Modern Graphics, Inc., Weymouth, Massachusetts

Printed on permanent/durable acid-free paper
and bound in the United States of America

Library of Congress Cataloging in Publication Data

Daly, Jay.
  Presenting S.E. Hinton.

  (Twayne's young adult authors) (Twayne's United States authors series ; TUSAS 528)
  Bibliography: p.
  Includes index.
  Summary: Discusses the life and works of well-known author S.E. Hinton.
  1. Hinton, S. E.—Criticism and interpretation. 2. Young adult fiction, American—History and criticism. [1. Hinton, S. E.—Criticism and interpretation. 2. American literature—History and criticism] I. Title. II. Series. III. Series: Twayne's United States authors series: TUSAS 528.

PS3558.I548Z64 1987   813'.54   87–7458
ISBN 0–8057–8203–6

for Eowyn

Contents

Preface

In April 1967 the Viking Press brought out a book called *The Outsiders,* by S. E. Hinton, and the world of young adult writing and publishing would never be the same. This is not an exaggeration. In more ways than one, *The Outsiders* has become the most successful, and the most emulated, young adult book of all time.

The situation was ripe, in the mid-sixties, for the arrival of something like *The Outsiders,* although no one knew it at the time. There had been a "young adult" genre for many years, dominated by books like Maureen Daly's *Seventeenth Summer,* dreamy-eyed stories of carefree youth where the major problem was whether so-and-so would ask our heroine to the prom in sufficient time for her to locate a prom gown. Or there were cautionary tales to warn us that, if we were not good, and we all know what "good" meant, we would never get to the prom at all.

Into this sterile chiffon-and-orchids environment then came *The Outsiders.* Nobody worries about the prom in *The Outsiders;* they're more concerned with just staying alive till June. They're also concerned with peer pressures, social status, abusive parents, and the ever-present threat of violence. What in the world was this? It certainly wasn't the same picture of the teenage wonder years that the "young adult" genre projected (and no one ever lived). Welcome to real life.

There is a perception now that *The Outsiders* was published to immediate teenage accolades, but such was not the case. In fact, because the book was so different from what the publishers considered "young adult" material, it was at first sent out with the general trade, or adult, releases, where it disappeared into the murk. It was only gradually, as the word from the hinterlands drifted in, that the publishers realized the book was finding its word-of-mouth fame among the very teenagers whose lives it depicted. The rest, as they say, is history.

The grass-roots success of *The Outsiders* paved the way for writers like Paul Zindel, Richard Peck, M. E. Kerr, Paula Danziger, and Robert Cormier. It set off a wail of controversy from those who thought that there was enough real life in real life without also putting it into books. It caused many lesser writers to make the mistake of wandering off in search of the "formula" for her success, and it sent publishers scurrying off in search of other teenaged writer-oracles; everyone wanted a piece of "the next S. E. Hinton." In truth, of course, there is no formula, and it is not likely that there will be "another" S. E. Hinton.

There are now perhaps ten million copies of Hinton books in print. *The Outsiders,* itself now twenty years old, no longer a teenager, continues to be the best selling of all Hinton's books. Clearly there is more to this than the novelty of its publication in those pre-Hinton, Mary-Jane-Goes-to-the-Prom years. In fact there is something in *The Outsiders,* as there is in the other Hinton books, that transcends the restrictions of time and place, that speaks to the reader directly. It has nothing to do with the age of the author, and little to do with the so-called "realism" of the setting. It does, however, have very much to do with the characters she creates, their humanity, and it has everything to do with her honesty. Her characters are orphans and outlaws and, as the song says, "to live outside the law you must be honest." If there is a formula to S. E. Hinton books it is only this: to tell the truth.

There is also something that is quintessentially American about S. E. Hinton. Her books are all set in the real American heartland, the urban frontier, and her characters are American pilgrim-orphans, believers in the dream of perfection, of an American paradise on earth. Francis Ford Coppola, who filmed and cowrote, with Hinton, the screen versions of *The Outsiders* and *Rumble Fish,* called her "a real American novelist," straight out of the tradition that runs from Herman Melville right up through J. D.

Salinger, and beyond. The myth of the American hero, of the outlaw-individualist, of the "gallant," lives on in the eyes of Ponyboy Curtis and Johnny Cade.

None of this would matter, though, if it were not based on real characters. None of this would count if we did not believe that her books tell the truth, not so much about beer parties and gang fights, but about what it feels like to be a teenager, caught between childhood and adulthood, always on the outside looking in at a world that is very far from being a paradise on earth.

Chronology

1948   Susan Eloise Hinton born 22 July in Tulsa, Oklahoma.

1963   Enters Will Rogers High School, Tulsa, which will be the model for *The Outsiders*.

1964–65   Junior year, father's illness, writing of *The Outsiders*.

1966   Enrolls at the University of Tulsa, majors in journalism (later switches to education).

1967   *The Outsiders* published in April. Essay, "Teen-Agers Are for Real," published in the *New York Times Book Review* in August.

1968   Short story, "Rumble Fish," published.

1970   Graduated from the University of Tulsa with a degree in education. Writes *That Was Then, This Is Now* that spring-summer. Marries David Inhofe in September.

1971   *That Was Then, This Is Now.*

1975   *Rumble Fish.*

1979   *Tex.*

1982   Movie, *Tex*, released in September.

1983   Movie, *The Outsiders*, released in March. Son Nicholas David, born in August. Movie, *Rumble Fish*, released in October.

1985   Movie, *That Was Then, This Is Now*, released in November.

S. E. Hinton.
Photograph by David Inhofe.

1. Who Is This S. E. Hinton and Where Did He Come From?

Susie

First of all, S. E. Hinton is a woman. This is a fact that is known to most, but certainly not all of her readers, even at this late date, after the publicity of the movies, the photographs in national magazines, the announcement of the birth of her first child in the "Milestones" column of *Time*. Susan Eloise Hinton Inhofe is a woman.

The confusion persists because of the initials, but also because her books are consistent in the employment of first-person male narrators to tell the story. "I've always been a tomboy," she says, by way of explanation. Or, "I'm just more comfortable with that point of view. When I was young, girls never got to *do* anything. They got to rat their hair and outline their eyes in black, but that was about the extent of their activities. They got their status from what kind of car their boyfriends drove. Other than that they were . . . well, passive."[1]

Susie Hinton never had much of a desire to be passive. "I was a pretty good fighter when I was a kid." She was not a joiner in school, which is a little ironic in the author of books that talk so much about belonging. She was neither a greaser nor a Soc. She was in between or, more accurately, she was a true outsider. "I didn't have any label in high school. I think I was considered a little eccentric. I'm still considered a little eccentric. If I had a label at all it was probably something like 'The School Nut,' but I was friends with greasers, Socs, artsy-craftsies. I could talk to all of them because I wasn't any of them."

Hinton was born in 1948, although the myth that grew up around her has obscured most of the simple facts of her life, and she has done very little to help clear up any of the confusion that has resulted from it. Here, for example, are the "S. E. Hinton" entries in the *Author Biographies Master Index,* a book that gathers together references to short biographies of authors (these are indicated by the abbreviations following the name):

Hinton, S E	AuBYP SUP
Hinton, S E 1948–	WrDr 82
Hinton, S E 1949–	FourBJA
Hinton, S E 1950–	ChlLR 3, ConAu 81, SmATA 19, TwCCW 78, WrDr 80[2]

Either there are more S. E. Hintons around than we generally know about, or there is some confusion with dates of birth. Hinton has been known to begin question and answer sessions, by the way, with a comment like "There are three questions I will not answer: How old am I now, how much money do I make, and how's my love life."

She has a sister, Beverly, two years younger. Her mother is still living, in Tulsa, as is her grandmother, but her father, Grady P. Hinton, died of cancer (a brain tumor) when she was a junior in high school. He died while she was writing *The Outsiders.* It is not something she talks about, but one gets the impression that his hospitalization, and the inevitable, unavoidable conclusion that his illness promised, were factors in her withdrawing into herself. She spent much of that time alone in her room, or at the dining room table while her mother was away at the hospital, working on what became *The Outsiders.* "Susie was very close to her father," her mother has said "and I noticed that the sicker he became the harder she worked."[3] Susie Hinton was always an outsider.

Her interests were formed very early in life. She wanted to be a writer. "I always just plain liked to write, and I always liked to read. Part of the reason I started to write was to have something to read." For a time she also wanted to be a cowboy, "until I found out how hard it was." There are still times when she wonders whether she might not have given more attention to the cowboy prospect, had the writing not intervened so decisively. She is obviously more comfortable in Tulsa, with her family, than she would be at any New York cocktail party.

Her horse Toyota, who is eighteen years old at the time of this writing, is the model for Tex's horse, Negrito, in the book *Tex,* and her attachment to Toyota is echoed quite clearly in Tex's attitude toward Negrito in that book. One of her conditions for permitting Disney to film *Tex* was that they use Toyota to play Matt Dillon's horse in the film. She taught Dillon how to ride, maybe taught him too well. "Boy, that kid caught on quick. My horse loved him. He'd knock me down to get to that kid. It was irritating." She still considers Toyota's performance to have been outstanding, even among all the other fine performances, in the film *Tex.*

One of the things that has always puzzled interviewers is the way Hinton's interest and animation picks up whenever the subject of horses is brought up (usually by her, of course, not by the interviewer). Her normal demeanor is rather quiet and reserved. Her interviews are, in fact, remarkably similar to one another, from the early ones done after publication of *The Outsiders* right up until the latest. Her answers will often be verbatim repeats of earlier answers. In some ways this is a defense mechanism on her part, but it also reflects the level of boredom one must reach when perhaps five thousand different people ask precisely the same question (e.g., "Why do you write from a male point of view?") over the course of a relatively short period of time. Can anyone blame her if she perks up when the talk turns from one early love, now almost talked out of existence (writing), to another, virtually ignored (horses)?

Unfortunately, most interviewers don't want to hear about horses. So the carbon copy interviews (now including carbon copy movie anecdotes) remain the same, though recently, since the

birth of her son, Nick, she has shown a tendency to avoid traveling, so that the meetings and book events and conventions, and
other opportunities to repeat her lines have been reduced. This
is probably best for all concerned, anxious interviewer and shy
interviewee both. Susie will always be an outsider; she'll never
be the garrulous type, the hail-fellow-well-met who is good at
inteviews and talk shows. Just like the Susie Hinton of Tulsa's
Will Rogers High School in the sixties, she will not be found doing
things just because they are expected. She will, as she always
has, go her own way, regardless of what others think.

"The whole status thing drove me nuts," she says of her high
school years. "It drove me nuts that people would get ulcers over
who they should say hi to in the hall." It drove her to write *The
Outsiders,* which was in fact her "third first novel." A lot of writers
have two or three first novels; it takes a while to get the right
chemistry, and Hinton's first two "misfired" novels, while they
will never see the light of day, no doubt served their purpose. She
wrote *The Outsiders* during her junior year at Will Rogers (the
same year she managed to earn a grade of D in a creative writing
course) and, although the initial motivation for writing might
have been the "status thing," or some traumatic event ("A friend
of mine got beaten up one day, and it got me mad"), or even the
death of a boy ("a real boy like Dallas Winston was shot and killed
by the police"), the book had a life of its own and that is why it
continues to be read today. Meanwhile, Susie Hinton of Tulsa,
Oklahoma, who had always been a relatively shy and withdrawn
teenager, sensitive to criticism, became S. E. Hinton overnight,
"the teenage wonder," as she later put it, and—partly to protect
herself—she disappeared, in public at least, into the myth.

A Word about Tulsa

Before talking about the myth, we should say a word or two
about Tulsa, Oklahoma, where Hinton was born and has lived
most of her life. In a short autobiographical sketch probably written around 1972–73, she says of Tulsa that "there is nothing to

do there, but it is a pleasant place to live if you don't want to do anything."⁴ At the time, she and her husband, David, were living in California, where David was going to graduate school at Stanford, and it was understandable if she should sound a little condescending toward Tulsa. They had moved to Palo Alto shortly after returning from six months spent in Spain and Europe after the publication of *That Was Then, This Is Now,* but all that traveling was just an interlude, something you do when you have the chance, when you are young enough and free enough of other responsibilities to do it. Their roots, though, and their families, were back in Tulsa. They moved back in 1973, and they have lived there, either in the city itself or just south of it, in Bixby, ever since.

Tulsa, Oklahoma, is the setting for all the novels. Even when it's not the setting, it's the setting. *Tex* is set in Bixby, called "Garyville" in the book, but when Tex and Mason go into "the city," or "town," they're going into Tulsa. On the pay phone after being shot, Tex tells Cole Collins that he's "across from that big motel that looks like a castle," and that "big motel" exists, in Tulsa, down "where the interstate crosses the Ribbon." It's called the Camelot.

There are other real places, as well. The drive-in in *The Outsiders,* that's the Admiral Twin. Then of course there's Will Rogers High School; it's just as large and impersonal as any other high school in that kind of American city at that particular place and time (there were one thousand kids in Hinton's graduating class). And this is a clue to the importance of Tulsa in these books: it is both specific enough to make the setting real (even the normally California-centered movie people felt they had to shoot on location) and general enough to be representative of the kind of American city that is replicated, in dozens of cases, across the land.

Tulsa is a classic American city. It's got the river, the old railroad, the "good side" and "the bad side." It's got the new high rises downtown, and the half million or so population, and the problems of cities. Just outside, and all around it, are the wide open spaces of the Great Plains, reminders of the frontier past out of which all these American cities just suddenly appeared,

dark, dense spots in the prairie where people were drawn, almost
overnight in some cases, like iron filings to the magnets of the
railroad, or gold mining, or—in Tulsa's case—oil.

As late as 1905, Tulsa was still called Tulsey Town, "an un-
kempt frontier settlement where—in the words of one settler—
'we had to dodge roaming hogs, goats, and cows when crossing,
and sometimes wild animals would venture into the middle of
town.' "[5] Oil changed all that, and very rapidly. A big strike at
the nearby Glenn Oil Pool, the greatest high-grade petroleum
strike up until that time, made Tulsa an instant city. (Oklahoma
City happened even more quickly; it is described by one historian
as "the city which popped up out of the prairie between noon and
sunset on April 22, 1889.")[6]

Oil brought prosperity, work, and exponential growth. The city
drew a population of American individualists, frontier people,
people with vision and ideas for the future. The future was always
big in Tulsa, and why not. In this instant city, which knew of no
other century than the twentieth, there was no past.

There have been efforts to remedy this. A couple of small but
well-endowed museums have been established, primarily by rich
Tulsa oil families, to shelter regional art and history collections.
These are admirable, and said to be exceptional in their fields,
but they don't substitute for a real history. As with many American cities, particularly those in that great space of land between
the coasts, there is a kind of "orphan" character to Tulsa, a sense
of being left there, suddenly full grown, to fend for itself. Its
inhabitants, no doubt, participate in this orphan character as well.
The fortunate among them will create great Horatio Alger fu-
tures. That's the American way, the American Dream. Those not
so fortunate—and there are many more of these—will have a
harder time of it. They will tend to be the outsiders.

The Myth

Lou Willett Stanek, herself a teacher and author of novels for
young adults, has described an experience she had in 1967, when

she was directing a center for students gifted in English. It was from these "gifted" students that she heard "the first version of what is becoming the Susan Hinton myth." She continues, "I think I now know five, but originally I heard and told the students she was walking through a Tulsa park, saw a rumble, a young lad was killed, and Susan was so upset she ran home and started writing it out of her system."[7]

Other versions of the myth were that Hinton was herself an unreconstructed greaser, or that she was the "Voice of Youth," somehow captured alive and brought in from the heartland to murmur delinquent truths to which only she had access. Most of all, she was "the teenage wonder," the Real Thing in a world of tired imitations.

All these mythical Hintons were not very revealing of the real Susie. Even being "the teenage wonder" was not, for example, all fun and games. It put some pressure on her. That she felt this pressure keenly is reflected in the writer's block she suffered directly after publication of *The Outsiders*. It lasted over three years. "I couldn't even write a letter," she says. No, it was not all fun and games, but the myth helped.

First of all there was the mystery of the initials. What had been purely a marketing decision—to ensure that *The Outsiders* would get a fair reading at its introduction, and not be handicapped by those who would waste time wondering whether these tough-sounding boys could be authentic creations of a female author—the initials proved to be of more lasting value. Not so important any more as a disguise for the author's sex,[8] the initials are none-theless a natural protective device for an author who requires anonymity. "Success is like having your own cesspool. You know it's there, but you don't want to swim in it. I've had anonymity at home, and I've appreciated it."[9] Susan Hinton is a very private person, and, though it may sound contradictory, the myth helps protect this privacy.

The Myth of the Angry Young Greaser.

This was one of the early ones, a romantic notion of the young, unschooled rebel writing of social injustice, probably destined to die young in a motorcycle accident. Susie, in fact, was not a greaser—she was, and still is, unaligned. She was young, unschooled in that sense, but she was no genius primitive. As her later career will prove, she was as conscious of the requirements of craft in her writing as any student in a creative writing seminar, perhaps more so, because her success or failure was measured on a much broader scale (and was also, it would sometimes seem, more grudgingly given). Zena Sutherland writes of her initial meeting with Hinton, in January 1968, almost a year after *The Outsiders* was published, "Having learned that S. E. Hinton is a girl, I looked forward with curiosity to meeting her. Prepared for a tough, shrewd, and possibly belligerent young woman, I met a pretty, gentle, and slightly nervous girl."[10] She sounds surprised—as I suppose she was—that she was meeting the person, not the myth.

The Myth of the Social Commentator.

This might have been the easiest myth to subscribe to, given the lack of attention to anything but sociological interests in novels directed to young adults. Teenagers weren't capable of aesthetic judgements, this view held, but they could be damned troublesome on the issues. The importance of S. E. Hinton, then, was as a social critic, a look from the inside. Her books were not so much novels, stories, as they were status reports on the progress of teenage alienation and conflict between the social classes. The Tulsa papers carried columns by her on the subject of teenage delinquency and they even, amazingly, used *The Outsiders* as a call for the imposition of a curfew on people under twenty. (Hinton has had more than one lesson, over the years, on the relative powerlessness of authors over what people will do with their books.)

S. E. Hinton is a storyteller, however, not an anthropologist, though all the early interviews tried to make her one, and she went along for the ride. In reality, though, that kind of thing is best left to the Cherry Valances of the world; the S. E. Hintons have better material in the human heart.

The Myth of the Teenage Publication Machine.

This is perhaps the cruelest myth of all, given the extraordinary "sweat quotient" that goes into each Hinton book. Yet, because her books are so successful, the myth endures: S. E. Hinton, the Teenage Cottage Industry. Maybe it started with the idea that she cranked out a copy of *The Outsiders* on a school night after a fight in the park. Or maybe it had something to do with her admitted problem with spelling ("Editors take care of that for you," she says, as if she couldn't be bothered with such things in her slapdash rush to spew out the books). Or maybe it came about because of comments like these, in an early article published in a Tulsa paper:

> Her method of interrogating her sources and gaining their confidence would chill the blood of the most hard-bitten crime reporter.
> She carried a switch blade to gain their attention and to open a dialogue between the 'hoody' element she sought to understand and her Sunday school teaching self.[11]

This isn't true, either, not in any meaningful sense. None of this stuff is. She's no cold-blooded teenage book-making machine, and she's no genius primitive, either. The truth of the matter is that she, like most writers of fiction, works very hard on the mastery of her craft, for which there is no magic formula, no undercover work that will guarantee results, and there is never a guarantee that anything she writes will work at all. The myth is false; all these myths are false.

What they do provide, though, are masks, ways of protecting oneself from being hurt, armor such as the Motorcycle Boy would have worn. *The Outsiders* was such a personal book (they are all, of course, in their ways, personal books), and Susie was so young, that it would have been hard not to react emotionally to the public attention. She and her sister, Beverly, who was, at sixteen, two years younger than Susie and yet was along as her chaperone, went to New York, where she was interviewed in bookstores and on talk shows, her opinions solicited on subjects upon which she had never before been consulted. Letters began to pour in, and they were addressed to Ponyboy, and they were personal, from people who wanted advice or help, or who wanted her to join motorycycle gangs, or to be married (in more than one case), or just to talk. She read all of them; most were friendly but some not. She also read the critics and, particularly at that young age, she took each comment personally. She would, in fact, always take such comments personally.

Her preferred reaction was to retreat, but by then, after her editor, Velma Varner, and Viking Press had done the unusual thing, had actually published this novel by a teenaged author, it was too late to turn back. She could hide behind the myth, or the various forms of the myth, and she could do her best to write well, but she could not turn back. Staying gold, as Ponyboy Curtis discovered, was not possible in this life.

Hinton with Francis Ford Coppola.
Courtesy of the Tulsa Daily World.

2. *The Outsiders:* Staying Gold

> Space within its time revolves
> But Eve must spin as Adam delves
> Because our exile is ourselves.
> Archibald MacLeish, "Eve's Exile"

"When I stepped out into the bright sunlight from the darkness of the movie house, I had only two things on my mind: Paul Newman and a ride home." So begins—and ends—*The Outsiders,* published by Viking in April 1967, when Hinton was in her freshman year at the University of Tulsa. The sentence is a perfect frame for the narrative; it takes us at the end directly back to the beginning, where, theoretically, we may begin the story again. It's also a cute little trick to explain why the story was written in the first place: the entire book is a theme that Ponyboy must write for his English class. It's also symbolic, in its winding back into itself, of the private, insular world of the gangs. Most of all, it gives a sense of immediacy, a sense of being-there; it says that what we have been told is the truth of what happened, and only now will it be written down. It is also, because it has been done so often before, in too many forgettable stories, a cliché.

The sentence thus gives us a preview of the great strengths and weaknesses of *The Outsiders.* "Can sincerity overcome clichés?" one of the early reviewers asked, and the reader's answer to this question will determine the success of the book. There is much more of interest in *The Outsiders* than just sincerity and clichés, as we shall see, but our belief in the honesty of the storyteller is crucial. Without that, nothing else matters.

The story continues as Ponyboy is trailed home from the movie by a red Corvair filled with Socs (pronounced Sōshes — short for Socials—though let's face it, on the printed page it's "socks"), who jump him, but he is saved by his brothers Darry and Sodapop and other members of the gang, including Dallas Winston, the hard, tough guy, and Two-Bit Mathews, the frequently half-drunk joker with a switchblade. They are, because of their long hair, called greasers, and the greasers and Socs are sworn enemies.

Ponyboy, along with Dallas and Johnny, two other gang members, go to the drive-in that night, over the back fence so they won't have to pay, and there they meet two Soc girls, Cherry Valance and her friend Marcia. After the movie they are met again, this time in a blue Mustang, by a gang of Socs, including Bob Sheldon, "a handsome black-haired Soc," and a fight is averted only when Cherry says she will leave with Bob and his friends. Bob, it would appear from the many rings he wears, is the Soc who had earlier beat Johnny almost to death. Johnny knows this and it scares him but he refuses to run.

Ponyboy and Johnny go off to a vacant lot, stretching out on their backs to look at the stars and talk about their lives, Johnny about how his parents ignore him and Ponyboy about his parents' death in a car accident. They both wish for "someplace without greasers or Socs, with just people. Plain ordinary people." At last they fall asleep and wake up much later. Ponyboy rushes home to find his oldest brother, Darry, waiting up for him. They argue and Ponyboy decides to run away. He grabs Johnny and they get as far as the park, where they meet the blue Mustang again, and in the ensuing fight, Johnny stabs Bob and kills him.

Now they feel they must indeed run. Dallas gives them directions to a church hide-out, out in Windrixville, and they spend five days there, reading *Gone with the Wind* and eating baloney sandwiches until Dally (Dallas) comes for them, taking them into town for a meal, and Johnny states that he's not running any more. He wants to go back and turn himself in. On the way home, though, they pass the church and see that it is burning, perhaps as a result of cigarettes they left smoldering inside. There are children trapped in the church; Ponyboy and Johnny rush in to save them. They get the kids out, but Ponyboy is burned and Johnny is hurt badly, a heavy timber having fallen on his back.

The two boys are heroes, but Johnny is hospitalized in critical condition. Ponyboy visits him at the hospital and brings him another copy of *Gone with the Wind*. He visits Dally also, whose arm was burned pulling Johnny out of the fire, and Dally complains about not being able to come to the big rumble that is planned for that evening between the Socs and greasers.

The rumble proceeds on schedule, with the full cast of characters, including even Dally, who has used Two-Bit's switchblade to persuade the nurses to let him leave. The greasers win, and Dally and Ponyboy rush off to tell Johnny about it. When they arrive they find Johnny almost dead. "Stay gold, Ponyboy," he says, referring to a Robert Frost poem they had recited back in the church. "Stay gold."

Johnny then dies and Dally, for whom he had been perhaps life's only bright spot, can't take it. He rushes out and robs a grocery store, knowing the police will get him. Ponyboy and his brothers reach the vacant lot just as the cops surround Dally. Dally raises an unloaded gun at them and they fire, killing him.

Ponyboy collapses (a concussion from the fight) and spends the next week or two in bed. He doesn't want to believe that Johnny is dead, and he has also convinced himself that he, not Johnny, killed Bob. There is a hearing where he is acquitted without being allowed to confess, which he had intended to do. Nothing changes, though. He is still numb inside, breaking out of himself only to sympathize with Sodapop, when he learns that Sandy, Soda's girlfriend, has not kept faith with him. The numbness finally ends when he discovers a note from Johnny in their copy of *Gone with the Wind*. It's another plea to stay gold, and it breaks through Ponyboy's numbness to bring out the submerged emotion beneath. He decides to tell the story, using a semester theme assignment that has been hanging over his head. Picking up the pen he begins: *"When I stepped out into the bright sunlight . . . ."*

We don't know how Ponyboy's English teacher responded to his book-length semester theme, but the initial response of the book

review media was quite favorable. This is not to say that it was
uniformly favorable. If *The Outsiders* were to achieve what it set
out to achieve, a story about things as they were, not as some
wished them to be, it could hardly help offending those who did
not receive what they wished to receive. Some reviewers described
the book as "unconvincing," and the worst of them, *Kirkus Reviews,* a professional review publication, missed the mark so completely as to nominate Cherry Valance, the book's most cardboard
character, as the author's alter ego. *Kirkus* also won the prize for
Least Prophetic Review, ending with, "You can believe a teen-
ager wrote it but you can bet teen-agers won't believe what it
says."[1] After nearly two decades and tens of millions of readers,
The Outsiders continues to win that bet with hundreds of new
"disbelievers" every day.

Most of the reviews were a little more sympathetic. Thomas
Fleming, in the *New York Times Book Review,* asked our opening
question: "Can sincerity overcome clichés? In this book by a now
17-year-old author, it almost does the trick. By almost any stan-
dard, Miss Hinton's performance is impressive."[2] Fleming has
some problems with the book's melodrama and clichés, but for
the most part his judgment echoes that of his fellow critics, and
remains valid today. Jane Manthorne called it a "remarkable
novel . . . a moving, credible view of the outsiders from the inside."[3] Zena Sutherland also used the word "remarkable," noting
that it was "written with distinctive style by a teenager who is
sensitive, honest, and observant."[4] In *Library Journal* Lillian Gerhardt wrote that it was a "rare-to-unique" book and its author a
"writer not yet practiced in restraint perhaps, but nevertheless
seeing and saying more with greater storytelling ability than
many an older hand."[5] In a note at the end of her review, Gerhardt
appended the following: "The cover-up initials stand for Susan
Hinton, who wrote *The Outsiders* at the age of 17. The book was
read for review before this information arrived from the publisher
and the author's skirts didn't hang in the story. Compassion was
certainly evident throughout, but women have no corner on this
quality. In retrospect the obvious clue is that maybe only a girl
could broadcast, without alibi, the soft centers of these boys and
how often they do give way to tears."[6]

The critical reaction, then, seemed secure enough: sincerity wins; *The Outsiders* would be a success. And a success it was, but not without the continuing bother of controversy along the way.

Much of the discussion came about because *The Outsiders* grew to be identified with something called "The New Realism" in young adult writing. The term—New Realism—was added later, but the fear—that books for teenagers were getting a little too realistic for their own good—was beginning to be heard more and more frequently during the time after the publication of *The Outsiders*. Indeed there are many who fix the point at which young adult writing changed, and changed utterly—from the cautionary Mary-Jane-Goes-to-the-Prom book to the attempt at serious and authentic portrayal of life as it is—with the publication of *The Outsiders*. Such a radical change could not be expected to go unchallenged.

Hinton herself, it seems, added fuel to this tempest in the teapots of various school boards and townships with her *New York Times* article, "Teen-agers Are for Real," which argued that teenage readers needed fiction that was grounded in reality, their reality. "Writers needn't be afraid that they will shock their teenage audience," she wrote. "Earn respect by giving it."[7] Unfortunately, though perhaps most teenagers were not shocked by *The Outsiders,* there were some others who were, and in the ensuing battle respect was a commodity in short supply. The New Realism, including *The Outsiders,* soon became a battleground for parents, teachers, librarians, and readers on both sides of the question.

At its worst, this unhappy trend of New Realism was toward "problem" books, books devoted to "the Big D's" (Robert Lipsyte's phrase): death, divorce, disease, and drugs. Novels, in other words, about concepts, not people. In such a discussion *The Outsiders* became a story about Class Warfare or Teenage Violence (both heavy-duty concepts rating capital letters) and most of the other, more crucial qualities of the novel were ignored. Here also, it was the concept, not the people—not the portrayal of human hopes and possibilities—that was the subject of the debate.

The irony is that, while the debate team focused on the gangs and the violence, the smoking and the beer drinking—all dreaded evidence of the New Realism—the major thrust of *The Outsiders* had nothing to do with realism at all. The real message of the book is its uncompromising idealism. The real reason the book struck such a responsive chord in its young readers (and continues to strike that chord) was that it captured so well the idealism of that time of life. Of all the young adult novels of that period, *The Outsiders* is by far the most idealistic, the least concerned with the strictly realistic. In its search for innocence, for heroes, for that Garden of Eden that seems to slip further away as youth fades into adulthood, *The Outsiders* is a book for dreamers, not realists. And youth is the time of dreamers.

On its surface at least, *The Outsiders* is indeed a novel about the friction between social classes, in this case between the greasers and the Socs. It is also about the hunger for status, for a place in the pecking order, both inside and outside these groups. And it is about the violence that is so much a part of that particular place and time of life. These concerns are not, however, what make the book come alive. The book comes to life through its characters and situations, their almost painful yearnings and loyalties, their honesty. While parents and censors argued about violence and sensationalism, the readers responded to the characters, the people, like the young reader who wrote in a letter addressed to "Mr. Hinton," "If you are really Ponyboy, and you have been through these ordeals, God must really love you."[8]

With all the talk of clichés and melodrama, why does this book continue to speak to new generations of young readers? Idealism alone, after all, is not enough. Nor is sincerity. Think of all the sincere, idealistic books in dustbins and yard sales around the country. The continuing popularity, the continuing interest derives, I think, from the fortunate combination of achievements by the young Susie Hinton in three essential categories: the hand of the storyteller that Lillian Gerhardt recognized; the continuing credibility of the characters; and the honesty, the sincerity already mentioned, embodied in the themes of the book, each of which reduces, finally, to the yearning to "stay gold."

The Storyteller's Hand

"Remembering. Remembering a handsome, dark boy with a reckless grin and a hot temper. A tough, towheaded boy with a cigarette in his mouth and a bitter grin on his hard face . . . ." Bob the Soc and Dallas Winston. Ponyboy's story is a memorial, and one can imagine the sixteen-year-old Susie Hinton, upset with the madness of the social sparring at her high school and the death of a boy not unlike Dallas Winston, beginning her story with much the same motivation. "I decided *I* could tell people. . . ."

This is the urge of the storyteller, the urge to communicate. In a novelist it is also the preliminary urge to get it all down, to preserve the story. I say preliminary urge because the novelist/storyteller also brings a later urge to bear on the story: the urge to embellish, to invent. Despite the confessional tone of *The Outsiders,* the story is, of course, for the most part invented. It is some measure of Hinton's success that we need to point this out at all.

The action of the story continues nearly nonstop, pausing occasionally to look at the stars, or to talk about southern gentlemen, but only for a short time before rushing ahead. Much of the action is violent, often described vividly, sometimes melodramatically. "Someone put his hand over my mouth, and I bit it as hard as I could, tasting the blood running through my teeth." You don't get much more vivid than that.

For the most part, though, the violence fits. The descriptions are believable; the scenes seem right. Hinton appears to have known instinctively how to balance introspection with action in just the proper measure to keep the reader hooked. She has often said that she wrote *The Outsiders* to give herself something to read other than the banal Mary-Jane-Goes-to-the Prom books she found on the library shelves. Her concern for the reader, for the velocity of the story, is apparent throughout. The plot leapfrogs from action scene to action scene; Hinton is not, at this stage of her career, comfortable in permitting introspection, even as it reveals character, to occupy the stage alone for very long. She wants things to *happen,* and happen they do, but there remains an inevitability to the story that saves it from being merely a recounting of a succession of fist fights.

S. E. Hinton calls herself a "character writer . . . I can't plot my way to the Safeway store." This is to understate the very crucial role that character plays in the unfolding of any plot. Plot without character is a lifeless thing, an artificial journey. The plot of *The Outsiders* is not the series of fights and rumbles; it is the characters' response to these events. Hinton has said, "While I was writing *The Outsiders* I'd do things like, go to school and say, 'Hey, I'm writing this book and this is what's happened so far, what should happen next?' And they'd say something like, 'Well, make the church burn down,' and I'd say, 'Oh, that sounds good,' and I went home and made the church burn down."[9] This is the perfect example: that the church burned down is, in itself, meaningless; what the characters do about it drives the story to its inevitable end.

All of this is firmly in the tradition of American storytelling. Place the character in the crucible of some extreme situation, put him (it has been, traditionally, nearly always *him*) on the frontier, on the big river, on the New Bedford whaler, and see what individual acts of valor or cowardice he will perform. "ACTION IS CHARACTER," F. Scott Fitzgerald wrote in the notebooks for his final, unfinished novel, *The Last Tycoon*. ACTION IS CHARACTER, an equation that would not have been lost on young Hinton (who, after all, claimed Fitzgerald as an influence early on in her career).

ACTION IS CHARACTER makes two demands, really: that character be revealed (not stated) through action, voice, response to enforced situations; and that the action of the story must itself, at least in part, grow out of the character of the individuals involved. In *The Outsiders* it is instructive to see how these demands are met in some cases, nearly met in others, and, in at least one case, tantalizingly ignored.

The Characters

The Curtis Family.

The story centers on Ponyboy and the Curtis Family, three brothers orphaned by the death of their parents in a car crash eight months earlier. Because they are so central to the story, and because of the internal dynamics of the family, they form, in some respects, a separate character study. Darry, the oldest, has assumed the role of father, a role with which he is not entirely comfortable. He is deeply concerned about the possibility of a family break-up and, to prevent this, he feels he must hold his younger brothers, Ponyboy in particular, to high standards of behavior (which, in his view, include getting good grades in school, not smoking in bed, and staying out of trouble with the law). Darry, who Ponyboy eventually realizes has "a silent fear . . . of losing another person he loved," tries to guide this group of orphans with a firm hand. At the same time he's guiding them, he can never entirely escape the fact that he's one of them. As a result, the Curtis household under Darry's leadership provides some of the book's more colorful scenes:

> We all like our eggs done differently. I like them hard, Darry likes them in a bacon-and-tomato sandwich, and Sodapop eats his with grape jelly. All three of us like chocolate cake for breakfast. Mom had never allowed it with ham and eggs, but Darry let Soda and me talk him into it. We really didn't have to twist his arm; Darry loves chocolate cake as much as we do. Sodapop always makes sure there's some in the icebox every night and if there isn't he cooks one up real quick. . . . I don't see how he stands jelly and eggs and chocolate cake all at once, but he seems to like it.

Orphans leading orphans; it sounds like chaos but it also sounds like fun.

Ponyboy, who at fourteen is the youngest, spends the entire first half of the book bridling under his brother's discipline (long after we have seen that Darry's love and concern are obvious). "Darry's hard and firm and hardly grins at all," is how Ponyboy describes him on page ten. Ponyboy, whose voice is so authentic and sincere throughout the book, slips out of character only once, when Cherry Valance asks him about Darry. "Is he wild and reckless like Soda? Dreamy, like you?" Ponyboy lashes out at Darry, "He's hard as a rock and about as human . . . he can't stand me," but no one believes him and, out of frustration, he does the one unforgivable thing, the one out-of-character thing: he takes it out on Johnny Cade. "An' you shut your trap, Johnny Cade, 'cause we all know you ain't wanted at home, either. And you can't blame them."

Two-bit slaps him "a good one across the side of the head" and Ponyboy says something very close to "Thanks, I needed that." The outburst is so out of character that it might as well have been hysterical. By this time in the story the reader is a little sick of Ponyboy's blindness to his brother's love for him. It isn't until page 106 that Ponyboy owns up. "Suddenly I realized, horrified, that Darry was crying." He admits only then that he knows how much Darry loves him. "I wondered how I could ever have thought him hard and unfeeling." This is hard to swallow as an epiphany. The reader mostly wonders: what took him so long?

Ponyboy's resistance to Darry rankles early on, because it is too insistent, too disdainful of the evidence against it. (His change of attitude toward Dallas Winston, whom he claims to hate at first, then comes to have a more complicated opinion of, is much more interesting.) One thing it does do, though, is to set up a crucial, and nicely brought off, family triangle, with the middle brother, Soda, literally in between, "the middleman in a tug o' war."

Soda is sixteen, going on seventeen. He seems to be admired by all who know him, nearly idolized by Ponyboy. "Soda is different from anybody," Ponyboy says. "He understands everything." He looks "like some Greek god come to earth." "He gets drunk on just plain living. And he understands everybody." In a later description Soda reminds Ponyboy "of a colt. A long-legged palomino colt that has to get his nose into everything." Hinton sets up Sodapop in much the same way that the world has set him up. He's handsome as a Greek god; he's reckless and natural; he's the model of understanding; he's out for fun and he generally finds it. He even has a girlfriend, Sandy, with "china-blue eyes," whom he loves and wants to marry. He's one of those blessed people who don't have to think too much and for whom life will always show its sunniest side. Except that, suddenly, he's not.

Soda's character, which had been flat enough for us to ignore, suddenly opens up and blossoms, like a small flower, with the revelation of his loss of Sandy. It all happens off-stage, and without anyone's notice, because in this family drama he is too involved with keeping the polarities of Darry and Ponyboy apart (and together) to feel his own sadness worthy of notice. If the antipathy of Ponyboy and Darry is overplayed, the good human character of Sodapop is coaxed out with a subtlety that leaves the reader as surprised and penitent as the two brothers.

The irony is that the author seems to have tried very hard to set up the artificial antagonism of Darry and Ponyboy. As a result, her hand is too visible; the characters seem manipulated. Sodapop, on the other hand, seems almost like an afterthought, someone to fill up the space between the two antagonistic brothers. There is no sense that Hinton is trying very hard with Soda at all. Consequently, when he quietly blossoms at the end of the book, he seems to do it all on his own.

Ponyboy Curtis.

Of all the characters in all the Hinton books Ponyboy Curtis remains number one in terms of reader identification. While on the surface this may appear to be a sign of an exceptional literary creation, unfortunately, most often it is not. Most often it is the sign of an easy character, a safe character, an individual who takes few risks and consequently alienates few readers. The most successful characters, on the other hand, must take risks in order to achieve a fullness of independent life. This must seem a heresy, to suggest that Ponyboy, who is such a popular character, who has such a legion of different readers who all say, "he speaks for me," is something less than perfect, but the fact is that only politicians on the election trail claim to speak for everyone, and the best literary creations are rarely politicians. Ponyboy, though he struggles awkwardly sometimes to emerge as a fully developed character, suffers from this fate: he's just a little too much the literary politician; he tries too hard to put chickens in everybody's pot.

Some of this criticism comes about because of the requirements of his position as narrator. He must tell the story and—particularly in this book—he must appear to be scrupulously honest and forthright. And in this he is successful. In a sense he sacrifices his own complexity of character for the greater goal of the book's sincerity. His voice generally seems so earnest and clear and acceptable that he almost disappears. At its best it's like the voice you hear in your head when you are reading at night: it's your own voice but it's also that of the character in the book. The two tend to merge. It's a kind of paradox: reader identification may become so strong that the character disappears.

Ponyboy may be sacrificing his complexity for a higher goal, but he pays too high a price. Hinton's later first-person narrators (particularly Tex, and Rusty-James in *Rumble Fish*) are more successfully rendered; they succeed in both relating the story and emerging as independent, living beings. They are people different from ourselves, which, from the artist's point of view, is the object of creation. This is not to say that Ponyboy is an utterly failed characterization (he's not; in fact he seems to have more of a presence after we have finished the book than he does while we are reading it) but he is simply less interesting, less complex than his later counterparts. In fact he's not even the most interesting character in *The Outsiders*.

The reason for this is that he does his job too well. Like a child under the apron strings of his storytelling role, he seems unable to break free into truly independent action. The one time he acts surprisingly, his lashing out at Johnny Cade, seems less an indication of his human complexity than it does a simple author's error. It grates on the reader; it doesn't amplify the character.

Compare him to Rusty-James. Rusty-James performs the function of first-person narrator, the voice in the mind, but he distinguishes himself absolutely as a voice in his own right. While the reader may identify with Ponyboy, nobody truly does that with Rusty-James. They feel for him, they like (or dislike) him, they pity him, they grieve with him, but they don't identify with him. That's what makes him a successful character.

Again, it's not that Ponyboy fails as a character. If he did, the scene where he takes his anger out on Johnny wouldn't seem such a gaffe, and his blindness to Darry's love wouldn't rankle so much. It's just that he suffers in comparison with some of the later first-person narrators, perhaps because he is much more the unfiltered voice of the young author than the later characters, who spring from a much more seasoned pen. In his favor, though, is the indisputable fact that, without the eye of this character, his descriptive insight, and his credibility, there would be no book. When we talk of the book's sincerity it's Ponyboy's sincerity we mean. The problem is that he is too easy for us to believe in, too sure and predictable a voice. When he chooses to enter the burning church to save the children it is absolutely in character; there is no doubt in our minds what he will do. It is not an action that reveals character; at best it verifies character. With Dallas Winston, on the other hand, there is no such guarantee.

Dallas.

In William Blake's poem *The Marriage of Heaven and Hell,* Blake wrote of the poet of *Paradise Lost* that "the reason Milton wrote in fetters when he wrote of Angels & God, and at liberty when of Devils & Hell, is because he was a true Poet and of the Devil's party without knowing it."

In similar fashion Hinton, through the character of her narrator, Ponyboy, seems to approach what becomes her most provocative character creation in *The Outsiders,* that of Dallas Winston. By the end of the book we can't help but feel that she, and Ponyboy, are also of the Devil's party without knowing it.

Ponyboy describes him early on (page 18). "He had an elfish face, with high cheekbones and a pointed chin, small sharp animal teeth, and eyes like a lynx." This description—whatever its intent—recalls descriptions given by medieval witnesses to appearances of the Evil One, of the Devil himself. That pointed chin, those animal teeth. I wouldn't want to make too much out of this—particularly since there is evidence that the character of Dally was based on a real-life boy in Tulsa—but it remains a curious description, a curious choice of words. None of the other characters—not even Tim Shepard or Bob Sheldon, the Soc—is described in such unhuman terms. It's as if Ponyboy, and the author, need to put up defenses against Dally, like magic circles believers draw around themselves to keep out bad spirits.

Throughout the book Ponyboy feels it necessary to keep repeating, "I didn't like him (19)," "he scared me (84)," "He was dangerous (97)," and "I'd never liked Dally (132)," until it becomes very clear that Ponyboy's feelings (and the author's) toward Dally are much more complicated than he is willing to admit. Dally is in fact one of those characters who, no matter how hard an author works to rein him in, just simply refuses to be controlled. That he is doomed is apparent from the beginning, but in the meantime, in the space of the book's pages before his death, he will act as he wishes, and the author will have to learn to accept that. For a novelist, characters like Dally are troublesome, to be sure, but they are also likely to be the most memorable, the most successful creations.

Dally appears on the scene from out of a mythic past. (Only the Motorcycle Boy, of all Hinton's characters, is closer to myth and mystery than Dally, but the Motorcycle Boy has nothing of Dally's humanity.) He comes from "the wild side of New York and had been arrested at the age of ten. He was tougher than the rest of us—tougher, colder, meaner." He had known the organized gang wars in New York (the time of the gangs seems always to be a time that Hinton characters yearn for) and he'd "seen people killed on the streets of New York's West Side." His eyes were "blue, blazing ice, cold with hatred of the whole world."

Of all the orphans in the book, Dallas is the most estranged, the most alone. The wall of ice and hatred that he puts up is a defense mechanism of the most fundamental sort. As he says to Ponyboy later in the book, "You'd better wise up, Pony . . . you get tough like me and you don't get hurt. You look out for yourself and nothing can touch you." But by this time Dally's affection for Johnny Cade has made big cracks in his defenses and the walls are starting to come down around him.

The reader can see these cracks beginning to form early in the story. His caring for Johnny Cade is too real, too important to him; he's vulnerable, and a vulnerable character forced to live a credo he no longer believes ("nothing can touch you") has all the marks of a tragic hero. Johnny calls him "gallant," in the sense that the southern gentlemen of *Gone with the Wind,* riding into certain death, are gallant. Pony refuses to see this. He claims instead that Soda, Two-bit, and Darry are "more like the heroes in the novels I read." But Ponyboy's reasoning is suspect; he's ducking a confrontation with his own definition of heroism, and he continues to avoid this confrontation throughout the book. Despite his negative attributes, only Dallas possesses the combination of courage and self-abnegation that Johnny's gallant heroes require. The question is only when and how this self-abnegation will play itself out.

The tension between Dally's nihilistic credo and the increasing number of times this facade breaks down in the face of those he cares about (not just Johnny; Ponyboy also) makes certain that, for the reader, he is the character to watch. The reader's notion of heroism, along with Ponyboy's, is finally put to the test in the character of Dallas Winston. He has all the qualities needed, but he's complex enough that we can never be sure of him; we have to pay attention to see what he'll do next, and this is why he takes over the reader's interest during the course of the story.

So, what is the verdict, then, on Dally? Is he gallant, or suicidal? Is he a martyr, or a fool? We know how Johnny would have voted: gallant. Ponyboy's description of his death evokes scenes like that of James Cagney on the church steps at the end of the movie *The Roaring Twenties:*

> And even as the policemen's guns spit fire into the night I knew that was what Dally wanted. He was jerked around by the impact of the bullets, then slowly crumpled with a look of grim triumph on his face. He was dead before he hit the ground. But I knew that was what he wanted, even as the lot echoed with the cracks of the shots, even as I begged silently—Please, not him . . . not him and Johnny both—I knew he would be dead, because Dally Winston wanted to be dead and he always got what he wanted.

> . . . But Johnny was right. He died gallant.

Ponyboy later makes an apparent retraction of this statement ("Don't try to decide which one [Johnny or Dally] died gallant"), but the jury has already reached the verdict. Fool or martyr? Probably both; probably all "gallant" heroes are both, and Dallas is indeed—as Johnny Cade defines the term—gallant.

Johnny Cade.

Johnny is another problematic character. He starts out as a one-dimensional victim: "Johnny Cade was last and least . . . picture a little dark puppy. . . . If it hadn't been for the gang, Johnny would never have known what love and affection are." He remains, to some extent, the victim, the sacrificial lamb, throughout the book, but he also has resources—and commands a curious allegiance from those bigger and tougher than he—that make him much more interesting than the lost puppy he is said to be.

Like all the others he is an orphan. His parents are still alive, but that makes him no less an orphan. "I walk in that house, and nobody says anything. I walk out, and nobody says anything. I stay away all night, and nobody notices . . . I ain't got nobody." His family is the gang, as Pony tells him, but for Johnny, "It ain't the same as having your own family care about you. . . . It just ain't the same."

His small stature, and maybe also that lost puppy look of his, invite violence and he gets it, from his father, wielding a two-by-four to beat him, and from the Socs, who beat him nearly to death in an event that occurs before the time of the story, and whose attack in the park ends in the killing of Bob. The first beating made him almost crazy with fear. He "never walked by himself after that," and he arms himself with a six-inch switchblade. "He'd use it, too, if he ever got jumped again." And he does.

Johnny could have been a pathetic character, but he's not pathetic at all. In many ways he's physically tough ("I had seen Johnny take a whipping with a two-by-four from his old man and never let out a whimper"). He's petrified of being beaten again, but when he and Pony are jumped in the park, he holds his ground.

He's also sensitive, one of the few people Ponyboy can talk to about the stars and the sunsets. He holds everything together (with the help of *Gone with the Wind* and a lot of baloney) during the time they spend hiding in the church. And, of course, he's also a hero, saving the kids in the burning church, pushing Ponyboy out in front of him as the roof collapses.

He's gallant, too, in the same sense that he uses the term to describe Dallas. His saving the children is gallant, but his death is also gallant ("Stay gold, Ponyboy. Stay gold"), and his last letter to Ponyboy, found in their paperback copy of *Gone with the Wind* ("Tell Dally. I don't think he knows") is, in its spirit of concern for his friend, even as he knows he is dying, gallant.

An unlikely southern gentleman. But Johnny has other unlikely qualities as well. What are we to make of this loyalty, almost homage, that Johnny commands from the rest of the gang? At first it seems just a protectiveness, an instinct in the stronger to shelter the weaker ("the gang's pet, everyone's kid brother"), but the relationship is much more complicated than that. It isn't just Johnny who needs the gang; the gang needs Johnny. "We couldn't get along without him," Ponyboy says. "We needed Johnny as much as he needed the gang. And for the same reason." Two-bit says the same thing, "We could get along without anyone but Johnny." Why is this? Why is Johnny so crucial? And what is this "reason" Ponyboy speaks of?

It can only be that Johnny represents for them the innocence they have lost, the gold of the Frost poem "Nothing Gold Can Stay." For Dallas in particular, Johnny's golden innocence is the only ray of hope in his bleak existence. "Johnny was the only thing Dally loved." In this way, Johnny's existence gives them all hope, gives them all a chance at redemption (coincidentally, no doubt, his initials are J. C.). The gang is a family (this is Ponyboy's "reason"), and just as it needs its father-figure (Darry), its nurturing mother (Soda), its black sheep (Dally), its straight arrow (Ponyboy), its cut-up (Two-bit), so it needs its child, its infant, to remind them that life, with all its bleakness and chaos, is, somewhere underneath it all, golden. Johnny Cade is that reminder.

Cherry Valance.

S. E. Hinton has been accused of a failure to render believable female characters and the character of Cherry Valance does little to dispute that charge. Her cardboard characterization is the book's major disappointment.

Our disappointment with Cherry is all the more keen because she seems at first to have such potential. She's presented as intelligent, pretty, sensitive enough to share sunsets with Ponyboy, caring enough to help bridge the gap between Socs and greasers—but when push comes to shove, she turns into a walking signboard ("Things are rough all over") or a nattering hypocrite ("Ponyboy . . . I mean . . . if I see you in the hall at school or someplace and don't say hi, well, it's not personal or anything, but . . . "). It's just impossible to believe that Cherry, the Social Philosopher holding forth in textbook tones on the meaning of values, the myth of social standing, the hopelessness of the rat race, and the beauty of sunsets, could be the same person who says, "well, it's not personal or anything," or even worse, "I could fall in love with Dallas Winston . . . I hope I never see him again, or I will."

It's hard not to feel betrayed by Cherry (real name: Sherri) Valance. If action and character are so intimately intertwined, and so vital in making fictional characters live, then Cherry demonstrates what happens when these two demands are ignored, when character is superimposed rather than allowed to grow from within. We keep waiting for her to make some surprising move, something that will startle Socs and greasers both, but she doesn't. Instead she remains her half-realized self, both too abstract a mouthpiece and too vacant and timid a social creature. Stretched at both ends, and without any strength of her own in the middle, she disintegrates, and then disappears.

One can only imagine that the character of Cherry Valance was a young author's revenge ("It drove me nuts that girls got their status from what kind of car their boyfriends drove") against a school full of status-seeking girls who ratted their hair (or ironed it, I suppose, if they were Socs) and thought about little else of importance in their lives. If so, then Cherry Valance really sticks it to them, but she wins that victory at the cost of sliding forever into the hazy background of the book.

Themes

As we've noted earlier, depictions of class warfare and teenage violence are to be found in *The Outsiders,* but they are not among the most interesting themes the book has to offer. Much more interesting (in ascending order) are three others. The first is the flip side of the class warfare theme, which we might call the Communion of Sunsets theme, the accumulation of evidence throughout the book that, beneath the trappings of madras or leather, individual hearts share much in common.

A second theme, though it's less a theme than an assumption, a set of circumstances that will recur in all of Hinton's work, is the Society of Orphans, the world of children, bereft of adult guidance, girding themselves to go it alone.

And the third, and most interesting, is that of Staying Gold, the theme of innocence and perfection, and of its ultimate equation with tragedy. A noble tragedy, perhaps, but an ineluctable one. All the talk of heroism in the book, and gallantry, is finally aligned with the inability of any of us to "stay gold."

The Communion of Sunsets.

"Maybe the two different worlds we lived in weren't so different," Ponyboy thinks, after meeting Cherry at the drive-in. "We saw the same sunset."

This was the first theme. This was the modest insight that prompted the young Susie Hinton to begin the book in the first place. In her talks to groups of parents and kids Hinton is fond of beginning with an anecdote about her high school at the time of *The Outsiders.* It goes something like this:

> The two extreme groups were the Socs and the greasers. Now, the Socs were so cool; they wore madras shirts and wheat jeans

and they were so cool, everybody wanted to be a Soc. They did cool things like go out and get drunk, and beat each other up, and go out and have drag races. But they were so cool. Everybody hated them and everybody wanted to be one.

At the other end of the scale were the greasers. They stood down at the back end of the parking lot, and they wore black leather jackets and blue jeans, and they were just the hoods of the school. I mean, it was just disgusting. They did hoody, scummy things like go out and get drunk, and beat each other up, and go out and have drag races.

Well, here were these two groups, doing the same things, in different parts of town, wearing different uniforms.

Susie Hinton, in a tradition of teenage aversion to hypocrisy that runs from Huck Finn to Holden Caulfield, could not abide such silliness. *The Outsiders* was her way of showing the lie.

The book begins with strict definitions of class separation: "the term 'greaser,' which is used to class all us boys on the East Side." And the Socs: "you can't win against them . . . because they've got all the breaks and even whipping them isn't going to change that fact." Gradually, though, these strict definitions begin to blur at the edges. "Did they cry when their boys were arrested?" becomes "It seemed funny to me that Socs—if these girls were any example—were just like us," and ultimately, "We saw the same sunset." It's not quite that easy, of course, and the two worlds can never completely merge, but the fact of their basic similarity, as people, becomes too obvious for anyone to ignore.

"I'll bet you watch sunsets," Cherry says to Ponyboy, and then she is quiet for a minute after he nods yes. "I used to watch them, too," she says, "before I got so busy."

The choice of sunsets to express this human similarity is a good choice. Not only are sunsets common property, and beautiful, they are also golden in the sense that the word is used throughout the book to suggest an unspoiled, untarnished closeness to life, to natural processes, that is a part of the birthright of everyone. Civilization, in the form of class restrictions and statusmongers, in the form of Cherry's busy-ness, interferes with this communion, but it only obscures it; it does not change it.

Sunsets, therefore, are reminders that, not only are class restrictions artificial and unnatural, so also are the day-to-day fences that all of us put up around ourselves equally manufactured and artificial. In *The Outsiders,* behind their fences, beneath their uniforms, all the characters share strains of common emotion and need. They are all, in the private sense, the outsiders of the book's title, orphaned by the requirements of class or status or image or self-defense or busy-ness from the ability to feel in their natural state. As Johnny puts it, "It seems like there's gotta be someplace without greasers or Socs, with just people. Plain ordinary people." The book's events show that he is right, that such a place exists, not out in the country, as Ponyboy imagines, but inside each of them.

The Society of Orphans.

Richard Peck was one of the early commentators to recognize that *The Outsiders* was "a story about belonging."[10] And belonging will remain a concern of all the books (unresolved, really, until *Tex*), because Hinton characters are all, in one sense or another, orphans. The Curtis boys are true orphans, but this orphan status extends beyond those whose parents have died to those who have been abandoned in other ways, whom we'll call "working" orphans. All the characters are either true orphans, working orphans, or of an uncertain family situation. The orphanage table might look something like this:

True	*Working*	*Uncertain*
Ponyboy	Johnny	Cherry
Sodapop	Steve	Randy
Darry	Bob	
	Dallas	

In the same way that the Curtis brothers, real orphans, circle their wagons and gather together to protect themselves from the disruptive hand of the state, so the other, working orphans look to the gang to provide them with the safe, warm acceptance of a family. The result is a Society of Orphans, where the outside (grown-up) world is walled out (and where its intrusions are usually cataclysmic) and where the idealistic, even severe, orphan values of the gang are preserved. In this way the outsiders become insiders. Socs and greasers, for example, have a lot more in common with each other than any of them has with any adult they might meet. Despite their class differences, they do, as Ponyboy might put it, see the same sunsets.

The orphans of *The Outsiders* are outlaws and dreamers. They're like "that tragic boy," Peter Pan, in J. M. Barrie's turn-of-the-century play. The Boy Who Would Not Grow Up. Peter Pan, and his group of orphans, the lost boys, rejected by their parents, make their own world of heroics and adventure. They have their own Never Land, where they belong. Wendy, like Cherry with her busy-ness, cannot prevent herself from changing, until she suddenly turns around to discover that she is "old, Peter. I am ever so much more than twenty."[11] Peter Pan, on the other hand, stays pure; he never grows up. He stays gold.

Likewise do the lost boys in *The Outsiders* form their own, more perfect world in the world of the gang. They dream of the perfection they know must exist, their Never Land, that perhaps they even once had and lost, where things are gold, where Johnny Cade can find his "ordinary people," where Ponyboy's parents remain golden and young. The striking thing about these orphans is that they use it to their advantage; they are dreamers and they use their abandonment to feed their dreams. Life intervenes, of course, and their dreams will never come true, but that's only because they have such high standards. They want perfection. Like Peter Pan, they want to stay gold forever.

Staying Gold.

The Outsiders, in comparison with those books to which it is usually compared, is a fairly literary book. By that I mean that there are repeated references to other books and literary works during the course of the story, references that are used to amplify the story itself. Ponyboy refers to Dickens's *Great Expectations,* "that kid, Pip, he reminded me of us," and, later, to "Jack London's books" when he is describing the rumble. There is also the continuing reference to Margaret Mitchell's *Gone with the Wind*. The general question of literary heroes receives its share of attention in the book. All of these are of secondary importance, however, compared with the Robert Frost poem "Nothing Gold Can Stay," recited by Ponyboy in its entirety.

> Nature's first green is gold,
> Her hardest hue to hold.
> Her early leaf's a flower;
> But only so an hour.
> Then leaf subsides to leaf.
> So Eden sank to grief,
> So dawn goes down to day.
> Nothing gold can stay.

Ponyboy recites this poem for Johnny on page 85. They are at the church, and have just been witness to a lyrical dawn: "All the lower valley was covered with mist, and sometimes little pieces of it broke off and floated away in small clouds. The sky was lighter in the east, and the horizon was a thin golden line. The clouds changed from gray to pink, and the mist was touched with gold. There was a silent moment when everything held its breath, and then the sun rose." The poem captures a feeling that is important to Ponyboy, though he's not sure of all of it. "He meant more to it than I'm gettin," he says, "I always remembered it because I never quite got what he meant by it." Ponyboy, who has the capacity to be a little slow when it serves to advance the story, needs Johnny to validate the poem for him, in his letter at the end of the book. *"[H]e meant you're gold when you're a kid, like green. When you're a kid everything's new, dawn. It's just when you get used to everything that it's day."* The only way to stay gold, then, is to stay a kid, or at least to retain that childlike wonder, that innocence, which continues to make the world new. The key to staying gold then, in Johnny's view, is to stay, like Peter Pan, a child.

If this is indeed the case, then it creates problems. To stay at a Peter Pan level of innocence is to be retarded (in all senses of

the word). All of us are in fact more like Wendy than like Peter;
we lose gradually that limber quality of youth, the idealism and
innocence, the ability, so to speak, to fly. To the extent that we
retain some of this capacity we are blessed, but to retain it fully
is impossible. Not just because "nothing gold can stay," but also
because it would be unnatural to do so. Innocence cannot escape
coming to terms with life, which does not necessarily mean being
corrupted. The opposite of innocence is—not corruption, of course—
but knowledge.

Worse yet, innocence/youth/idealism carried to such extremes
is not innocence/youth/idealism at all. It is usually a more selfish,
and sometimes dangerous, thing. Look at Ponyboy's selfish attitude toward Darry early in the book. This is an attitude that is
innocent of the most elementary awareness of another human
being. When he sees Darry cry, and feels his hurting inside, it is
suddenly a loss of innocence, a falling into knowledge of the real
world, but it's a far better condition he falls into than that he left
behind.

It is no accident that those literary heroes who stay gold, who
retain their innocence unnaturally, lead lives whose effect upon
others is often far from innocent. There is something inhuman
about them. Think of Melville's Billy Budd, or Lennie in Stein-
beck's *Of Mice and Men.* Their very innocence tends to lead them
always toward, in Lennie's words, "another bad thing." It's as if
they can't help but hurt people in the end. J. M. Barrie, once
again, at the end of *Peter and Wendy,* describes his creation Peter,
who would not grow up, as forever "young and innocent," but then
he also adds, "And heartless."[12]

The Frost poem is in fact not so much about the fleeting nature
of youth, or even life, as it is about the Fall. Notice those repeating
verbs, "subside . . . sank . . . goes down." The loss of Eden, of
that state of perfection of which the "gold" of the poem is but a
cruel reminder, this is the real knowledge in the poem, as it is
in *The Outsiders.* When Ponyboy remembers his parents, it is   ·
always in a kind of misty Garden of Eden setting: "I remembered
my mother . . . beautiful and golden, like Soda, and wise and
firm, like Darry." It's been only eight months since they died, but

already they seem to have entered into a golden mythology. The book's idealism invents that place "in the country" of sunsets and ordinary people, but in fact—after the Fall—such a place cannot exist, not in this life.

Which brings us to the one way of staying gold that works. It is the only way of achieving the perfection that was promised. It involves memory, and the shifting of emphasis in Frost's last line from "gold" to "stay." Nothing gold can *stay*. Rather than agree that Ponyboy's image of perfection cannot exist in this world, the book agrees only that it cannot stay here. By dying Johnny stays gold in a way he could never have achieved in life. Even Dally becomes a gallant in death, frozen in time forever under the streetlights of the park like a carved figure from Keats's "Ode on a Grecian Urn."

Most of all, Ponyboy's parents stay perfect parents in a world sadly lacking in parental perfection. They will be young and golden and love him always. His mother in particular remains "beautiful and golden," perfect in a way she could not have remained in life. It is an irony that only by abandoning him could she become for him that symbol of perfection that Ponyboy, and all the others, so desperately need. In the words of the Keats poem: "She cannot fade, though thou hast not thy bliss, / For ever wilt thou love, and she be fair!"

In the pages of *The Outsiders,* and in Ponyboy's memory, she remains, as the song goes, forever young. She stays gold. It's a cruel sort of perfection, but for the idealistic heroes of all the Hinton books (up until *Tex*), who prize perfection so highly, it's the only kind of Paradise they know.

Hinton autographing one of her books for a fan.
Courtesy of the Tulsa Tribune.

3. *That Was Then, This Is Now:* Time Is the Hero, and the Villain

> I was so much older then,
> I'm younger than that now.
>   Bob Dylan, "My Back Pages"

The Outsiders brought Susan Hinton a taste of success, an unexpected notoriety, a chance to travel a bit and visit places she might not otherwise have seen, and it brought her also one other thing she hadn't counted on: writer's block. "I couldn't write. I taught myself to type in the sixth grade, and I couldn't even type or use my typewriter to write a letter. Things were pretty bad because I also went to college and started reading good writers and I thought, 'Oh no.' I read *The Outsiders* again when I was 20, and I thought it was the worst piece of trash I'd ever seen. I magnified its faults: 'Oh no, this thing has got my name on it.' "[1]

In the time of excitement after *The Outsiders* came out, amidst some of the other speculation and misinformation, there was the suggestion of prolific output to come, of a "suit box" full of manuscripts. One newspaper article referred to not one but two works-in-progress. "One is about two boys on a ranch in Texas during 1847 and the other is about some teenagers on a modern dude ranch."[2] Needless to say, these have never seen the light of day.

More likely, the two manuscripts in the suitbox were the remnants of her earlier books "in training" for *The Outsiders*. "I'd

been in training for about eight years by the time I'd written it."[3]
There were in fact no firm plans for a new book. This is clear
from a remark quoted in the newspaper article that mentioned
the "suit box". "I have said about all I have to say about teen-
agers, then or now."[4]

This was not a very prescient comment, not from the "Teenage
Cottage Industry," anyway, but it reflects, I think, the fear that
she might have "said about all I have to say," period. (The curious
modifying phrase, "then or now," refers, it would seem, to the
1847 manuscript, though this is not clear in the article.) Having
spent a year at the University of Tulsa exposed to "good writers,"
she began to have doubts. Perhaps *The Outsiders* was a fluke, a
long shot that just happened to come in. Even worse, perhaps it
was also a not-very-good fluke, a horse that won only because the
rest of the field was so poor.

I don't think there is any doubt that Susan Hinton has always
been very serious about her writing, from the time she started,
however early that might have been. The kind of writer's block
she describes ("You just sit and stare at the keys until you start
sweating blood") doesn't happen to people who don't take the gift
seriously. All the publicity surrounding the "teenage wonder"
treated her as if she were some kind of noble savage, or—maybe
a better analogy—talking dog, where the news is not what the
dog has to say but rather that it can talk at all. Perhaps it was
unavoidable in that atmosphere to wonder if it wasn't just a passing, sideshow attraction. Maybe just a fluke.

We've all heard tales of writers being possessed by the spirit
of a character or an event and being somehow transported, carried
outside themselves, so that the story seems to take off on its own.
It sounds like a fable but indeed it is literally true. All writers,
in their peak experiences, seem at some point to have the impression that they are not in control, that they are mediums through
which someone else is speaking. It's a kind of blessed feeling,
maybe a little miraculous in its way, but it's not the sort of thing
that inspires overconfidence. No one—let's face it—will feel very
smug or relaxed who must depend upon the miraculous for the
delivery of everyday meat and potatoes.

It was natural, then, for Susan Hinton to begin to doubt the miracle. And everyone knows that the coming of miracles depends utterly upon the faith of believers. Without faith, the miracles will stay away, and they stayed away from Hinton for about three years, throughout her time in college. The one exception was the short story, "Rumble Fish," which was published in the University of Tulsa literary supplement, *Nimrod,* in the fall of her junior year.

During this fallow period Hinton kept a fairly low profile at the university. In her freshman year she changed her major from journalism to education, a move that reflects a genuine, lifelong interest in kids. (Part of the reason she has been able to continue to project that quality of honesty one feels in *The Outsiders* through all her later books is that she has not lost that quality herself.) But behind it all there remained the urge to write, which she had never—since the age of about ten, anyway—been without. She couldn't ignore it and her paralysis naturally had its effect: it made her depressed.

Luckily, she had support from others during this time, and a little push besides. Dr. Fran Ringold, a professor at TU, and the editor of *Nimrod,* gave her professional support. "She could articulate the creative process," Hinton has said. "I couldn't." If she couldn't articulate it, she was nonetheless living the downside of it, and the cycle was broken at last upon the insistence of her boyfriend (and husband-to-be), David Inhofe, whom she had met as a TU student. "He finally got sick of my being depressed and made me write two pages one day."[5] These two pages led to another two the next day, and so forth, until at last there was *That Was Then, This Is Now.* "David made me write *That Was Then, This Is Now.* When I was writing for fun, I loved it; when it turned into a profession it scared me. I kept thinking, 'You don't know what you're doing.' I wrote *That Was Then* over a period of three or four months, two pages a day, never looking back. David was my boyfriend at that time; if I didn't get my two pages done, we didn't go out."[6]

It may be that David's solution to writer's block (which also has a little something in common with the Greek play *Lysistrata*) is the only true solution. The miracles won't come back unless you make the way ready, and this requires work. Hinton, by this time, was ready for work. She seems to have approached *That Was Then, This Is Now* as if it were a challenge, almost an obstacle to be overcome. Her experience with "good" writing had increased over the years, and she knew that good writing involves more than unbridled flights of the imagination, that it is also something fashioned, formed, crafted. She knew, in short, that it involved discipline and work.

> So I was very careful with this book, and I wanted each sentence to be exactly right, and I'd just sweat out my two pages, and I'd put them in a stack, and I wouldn't even look at my two pages I'd done the day before. And finally I had a stack that looked like the size of a book, so I sent it off to the publisher.

> And I didn't have to do any re-write.[7]

That Was Then, This Is Now is, in nearly everyone's view, a much more disciplined novel than *The Outsiders*. From just our description of the story behind its composition, the word *discipline* stands out. Discipline is one way to fight the demons of self-doubt, and Hinton seems to have called up all the discipline she could manage in order to fashion a well-crafted book. As a result, we have something that is much more advanced, more mature, and better balanced than *The Outsiders,* that is more cool and studied and less emotional, but it lacks something. It lacks the spark, the élan vital that made *The Outsiders'* triumph over clichés so complete. *That Was Then, This Is Now* is simply a novel so "disciplined" that it almost seems wrestled with, brought by the ears to publication like a recalcitrant child. It's technically better, maybe, but it's not *better.*

At the same time we mustn't lose track of the fact that we are dealing with the work of a twenty-year-old author. In any other case we'd be cheering her future to come. Perhaps it's not fair, but the fact of the matter is that *The Outsiders* will always be treated like a precocious teenager while *That Was Then, This Is*

Now, scarcely older, will be held to more sophisticated standards. On the other hand, it's a tribute to the book that we happily apply these standards without giving much thought to the age of the author.

In that light, here is Hinton describing the experience of writing the book, during a talk she gave in 1980: "But I feel like the ending of *That Was Then, This Is Now*, where the narrator feels like he's just emotionally numb, he feels like he's just been wiped out, was the way I felt by the publication of *The Outsiders*. I just felt like it had drained me. So I got through that book, and I married my husand, and we went off to Spain to be hippies for a while."

That Was Then, This Is Now was an experience to be "got through," and she got through it. She learned from it that not all books would be as easy to write or as exuberant a writing experience as *The Outsiders*. In fact no other book would be that easy. *That Was Then, This Is Now* took more effort; she was able to exercise more control, and the result was a more controlled, a technically more admirable accomplishment, but it was not necessarily better.

That Was Then, This Is Now is a story of friendship, and of time passing, and of the gradual passing of friendship as well. Things change. It begins with Mark and Bryon, who is the narrator, in Charlie's Bar, a combination bar/poolroom near their home. Mark has lived with Bryon and Bryon's mother since his own parents killed each other in a fight, a scene he remembers vividly, since he was hiding under the porch at the time and witnessed it all. Charlie tells them that M&M ("the true flower child," Charlie calls him) has been looking for them and they go to find him. They arrive just in time to save him from a beating at the hands of Curly Shepard and his gang. Times have changed a bit since *The Outsiders:* the Soc-greaser rumble is a year in the past and, while there are still fights and muggings, it's not that clear-cut a division any more. And there are hippies now, long hair and peace medals, to confuse things further.

The next day Mark and Bryon go downtown to visit Bryon's

mother in the hospital (she'll be in and out of the hospital through-out the book, for unspecified reasons). At the hospital Bryon meets Cathy Carlson, M&M's older sister, who works in the snack bar. He doesn't recognize her at first, but when he does it becomes clear that he will see her again.

Bryon joins Mark upstairs, in the hospital room of a kid named Mike Chambers, whom Mark—at the suggestion of Bryon's mother—has been visiting. Mike is recovering from a beating he suffered when he was attacked by a group of black kids (he is white). He tells them the story behind his misfortune, a long, detailed story of his saving a young black girl who was being harassed by a gang of whites. After giving her a ride home he is pulled from the car by her friends, who assume that Mike is the reason she has been crying. He asks her to tell them the truth but instead she turns and says bitterly, "Kill the white bastard." So—as Mike puts it—they nearly do just that.

There are money problems in the household, with Mrs. Douglas in the hospital, and the boys search for jobs, without success. Charlie refuses to hire Bryon, because of his age, although there is also some question about his habitual lying. He does, however, offer to lend Bryon his car, so that Bryon can take Cathy to the dance on Saturday night.

At the dance they meet Ponyboy Curtis (whom Bryon doesn't like) and Angela Shepard, an old flame with a reputation befitting the Shepard family. Outside the dance Mark is hit on the side of the head by a bottle in a fight that Angela has stage-managed in order to punish Ponyboy, who has not responded to her romantic overtures. While Ponyboy was the target, it is Mark, naturally, who gets hurt. Bryon goes with him to the hospital, where the doctors patch up his head and send him home. The two boys renew their friendship, their brotherhood, in a long talk that night, their conversation loosened, on Mark's part anyway, by pain killers given him at the hospital.

Bryon takes care of Mark over the next few days. Their con-versations include a discussion of how things are changing. "That was then, this is now," is how Bryon phrases it, at one point. When Mark gets back to school he is almost immediately in trouble again, for "borrowing" the principal's car during school lunch hour. True to form, however, Mark talks and charms his way out of trouble.

They go to Charlie's the next night to try hustling a little pool. Bryon successfully hustles a couple of Texans, but the Texans are waiting for them outside as they leave the bar, with the object of teaching the boys a lesson or two about pool hustling. Charlie intervenes to save them, but in the ensuing fight one of the Texans shoots Charlie, killing him instantly. Bryon and Mark go through the next few weeks in a daze, trying to understand what Charlie's sacrifice means. Meanwhile, their money problems increase (Mom's sick again) and they confide in each other less frequently. Bryon turns more to Cathy instead.

Things change abruptly when M&M suddenly disappears. Cathy and Bryon spend a lot of time looking for him, without luck. Mark and Bryon pay Angela back one night for her part in the bottle fight by getting her drunk and shaving her head. Their relationship is deteriorating, though, and at times they snap at each other, often over something having to do with Cathy.

Angela's brothers catch up with Bryon and beat him senseless, but Bryon won't allow Mark to talk of revenge. Mark has meanwhile let it be known that he might have some idea where M&M is hiding, but by the time Cathy and Bryon finally find her brother he is in bad shape, hallucinating and terrified, under the influence of some powerful drug. They get him to the hospital, where the doctors do what they can but cannot assure them that he will ever fully recover. That night Bryon finds a cylinder of pills beneath Mark's mattress, too many pills for just a user. He calls the police and turns Mark in.

Mark doesn't even try to defend himself at the trial. He's given five years in the state reformatory. Bryon turns numb, turns away from Cathy, from everybody. Later, when he goes to visit Mark in prison, Mark tells him he hates him. Bryon thinks that if he could have, Mark would have killed him then and there. As the book ends Bryon is numb and "worn out with caring about people." In the book's last sentence he laments, "I wish I was a kid again, when I had all the answers."

The critics, for the most part, were laudatory. The book was voted one of the "Best Books for Young Adults," an honor it certainly deserved. In retrospect, though, one wonders whether some of this rather understated affirmation was not really a belated climbing-on-the-bandwagon of *The Outsiders?* After all, *The Outsiders* was— as they say in the Public Relations trade—"huge," and this one was clearly the more accomplished job. So what if nobody exactly understood what was going on. For example, here is the entire description of the book that accompanied its listing in "Best Books for Young Adults, 1971": "In this sequel to *The outsiders [sic]*, Bryon and Mark at sixteen are still inseparable, but Bryon is beginning to care about people while Mark continues to hot-wire cars, steal, and do things for kicks."

This, don't forget, comes presumably from someone who thought the book was one of the best of the year. It is not very accurate. First of all, to call it a sequel is a little misleading; it's not a sequel, really, not in the usual sense of the term (continuing a story begun in an earlier work). The two books share Ponyboy and the Shepards, in cameo appearances, but the story of Bryon and Mark is a wholly new invention; it has precious little to do with what happened in *The Outsiders*. When it does refer to the time of that earlier book, it does so not to continue anything but rather to contrast: that was then, this is now.

As far as the rest of the description goes, is that what happened? Bryon—the softie—beginning to care, and Mark—the madcap car thief—partying as usual? What about the betrayal? What about the drugs and the violence-shattered lives? What about the bitterness and the collapse of friendships and love affairs? What about the character Bryon Douglas, who is not "beginning to care about people" at all, but rather is "worn out with caring about people" in his own words at the book's end? Is this the same Best Book?

No matter. Probably it would have been in bad taste to describe accurately this problematical book in what was meant to be a commendatory listing. Unfortunately, the tendency to enshrine

That Was Then, This Is Now without looking too deeply is a trait shared by most of the more lengthy reviews as well.

Library Journal called it an "excellent, insightful mustering of the pressures on some teen-agers today, offering no slick solutions but not without hope, either."[8] If you look closely you'll notice the slight sociological bent that infected much of the critical reaction to young adult books of that time (and still does, to be sure). Problems and solutions. It was as if the reason for the existence of these books was not the quality of the writing, or the truth of the characterization, but rather the degree to which the book contributed to the solving of the youth "problem." A good book had all the right "problems" present and accounted for; if it not only had the problems but also resisted "slick solutions" it was undoubtedly high art.

Another, more obvious example of the sociologist/child psychologist school of literary criticism, so typical, was the review in *Booklist*. "Although the author offers no solutions to the problems of mixed-up youth and does not sufficiently develop the idea that caring what happens to others makes one vulnerable to being hurt, the realistic, first-person story will appeal to younger teen-agers."[9]

Most of the other reviews were quietly laudatory and safe. The *Publisher's Weekly* review said: "Drugs are now the scene in her newest book that retains the same background"[10] (as opposed, apparently, to whatever the scene is in her newest book with a slightly different background). There was really very little in-depth response. In general the reviewers seemed unsure, and perhaps a little intimidated.

Sheryl B. Andrews, in the *Horn Book Magazine,* seemed to dislike the book but could not quite bring herself to say why. She called it "disturbing" (a word Hinton herself would use to describe it, ten years later), and "sometimes ugly," but in the end she retreats to the safe haven of the sociologist-critic position: "but it will speak directly to a large number of teen-agers and does have a place in the understanding of today's cultural problems."[11] This is faint praise indeed.

Zena Sutherland, who has been for some time one of the most
perceptive and generous critics of writing for young adults, wrote
a short but strong review in her column on children's books in
the *Saturday Review*. Bryon, she wrote, "tells the story with the
same directness and honesty that made *The Outsiders* so ap-
pealing."[12] Once again, the reader's belief in the voice of the narrator is crucial, as it was in *The Outsiders,* and for Sutherland
that belief is rewarded. She also does not shirk the betrayal issue,
so important, so unavoidable really (though most of the other
reviewers managed to avoid it) if we are to have any sense of
character for Bryon at all. For Sutherland the betrayal is an
intellectual decision on Bryon's part, a conscious choice to be
fiercely true to his personal standards and, in some way, also to
protect himself. "[Bryon] hates himself for the betrayal of his
friend, but he's been a tough kid on the fringe of delinquency and
he's aware of what happens beyond that fringe. The situation is
harsh, yet the story has no minatory stridency. The writing has
perception; the characters are wholly believable."[13]

It's curious; so much of that is true, but the part about Bryon's
motivation for the betrayal, that he knew what happened "beyond
the fringe," is not sufficient. Sutherland included *That Was Then,
This Is Now* in her own book, *The Best in Children's Books,* published in 1973 (*The Outsiders* is in there, too). She notes the "bitter
realism" of the book, with "far more shock value than a treatise
on addiction," and she says of Bryon: "Heartsick, he rejects Cathy,
'worn out with caring about people.' "[14] To tell the truth, there is
certainly room for doubt about the "worn out with caring about
people" line; Bryon's history of caring about anyone other than
himself is so short that it seems unlikely he could have tired
himself too much. In fact, when Bryon says that of himself, on
the very last page of the book, it could easily be taken as an irony,
as yet another example of his ability to lie to anyone, himself
most of all. As Charlie said of him, "I trust your actions, but I
double-check most of your statements." This seems a wise move
on Charlie's part.

One other review worth looking at is Michael Cart's piece in
the *New York Times Book Review*. Like Zena Sutherland, Cart

admired the book and noted its "many similarities" with *The Outsiders*. He was right on target when he identified "the antagonist in this more ambitious novel [as] time," and he was on the right track when he stated "her theme: growth can be a dangerous process."[15] But he also found fault with the book, particularly at the end, "when love and hate have run their course, [and] all that is left to Bryon is not honest and believable grief but life-denying self-pity." This is a strong charge, suggesting, by implication, dishonesty and un-believability. When directed toward a fictional character, these are fightin' words.

As to Bryon's motivation for the betrayal, Cart evidently saw black where Sutherland saw white. "[Bryon's] central decisions—turning Mark in to the police and breaking off with Cathy—are made not intellectually but emotionally." Where Zena Sutherland saw evidence of a cool calculation to stay away from "the fringe," Michael Cart perceived a more personal and emotional trigger. They can't both be right. (But they can both be wrong.)

Themes

Time and the Inevitability of Change.

Time and change play a formidable role in the book. They join to form Michael Cart's statement of the book's theme: growth can be a dangerous process. Dangerous but necessary. It seems almost an attempt to repudiate the "stay gold" message of *The Outsiders*. It is as if Hinton—so sensitive to the faults of *The Outsiders*, the emotionalism and the apotheosis of youth—made a conscious effort to go the other way. You want discipline? Here's discipline. You want realism? Here's realism.

That Was Then, This Is Now turns the Peter Pan vision of the world inside out, and chooses instead to inspect the more unhealthy side of eternal youth. Times change, the book says; grow with them or be left behind. It's a brutal and unsentimental message and, as the events of the story prove, the rejection of idealism, the hardheaded choice to move on, may not be the real answer, either. The events imply that changing may not be very much better (other than the gift of staying out of jail) than staying behind.

Hinton has found, in her letters and talks over the years, that no other book has provoked the kind of discussion of motives and personal disagreements about character that *That Was Then, This Is Now* provokes. It is not a book that comes to a very comfortable conclusion. She made hard choices, herself, in composing the book (that discipline, again) and the reader must make some hard choices, as well.

The preoccupation with time and youth and change is a restatement of the Peter Pan dream; it was such a part of *The Outsiders,* such an idealistic and winning attitude of that book's most inspired characters, that it is not unexpected, surely, to have it make a new appearance in the next book. What is a bit surprising is the new attitude of the author toward it. All the boys in *The Outsiders* who will not grow up are given a lesson in acceptable behavior by *That Was Then, This Is Now.* We saw earlier that eternal youth, staying gold, was an impossibility, perhaps even a condition that was best left unrealized. *That Was Then, This Is Now* attempts to show why.

Mark is the Peter Pan holdover from *The Outsiders.* He's the one with the youthful, nothing-can-touch-me attitude toward life. "Mark always came through everything untouched, unworried, unaffected." He's the "innocent lion," with the Peter Pan view that the world is made for flying, not for worrying. Bryon is defensive; Mark is puzzled that anyone would need such an attitude.

> Bryon: "Pow! Care about somebody, give a damn for another person, and you get blasted. How come it's like that?"
>
> Mark: "You got me, Bryon. I never thought about it. I guess 'cause nothin' bad has ever happened to me."

This, don't forget, from someone whose parents have murdered each other in a scene that adds a point or two to the old charge of melodrama, still alive and kicking from *The Outsiders.* "Nothing bad has ever happened to me." Peter Pan, all the way.

Dallas Winston got to be Peter Pan, as did Johnny Cade, and so even—at least in desire—did Ponyboy, but Mark is not permitted that grace. In *That Was Then, This Is Now,* Mark is the avatar of youth, an exalted station in *The Outsiders* but an honor that has since lost much of its glow. Mark delivers the message, one of the unmistakable messages of *The Outsiders:* "You gotta just take things as they come, and quit trying to reason them out. Bryon, you never used to worry about things. Man, I been gettin' worried about you. You start wonderin' why and you get old." Sounds like Peter Pan talking to Wendy. And he failed to make his point with her, too.

Bryon keeps talking about how he is growing, changing, even maturing, but he is never completely convincing. He talks a good game, but he just doesn't yet know how to live it. "Do you ever get the feeling that the whole thing is changing?" Mark asks, and Bryon agrees, but the change, and—more important—their response to it, is out of their hands. They're powerless, finally. Both of them give up.

There is another concern relating to time that will be developed more fully in *Rumble Fish* but which makes a brief appearance here. This is the sense of nostalgia, the looking back to a past "golden age" for inspiration. Typically, this is the time of the gangs, the heroic time. Mark says of the gang, "We were like brothers. . . . We woulda died for each other then. And now everybody's kinda slipped away, and then we woulda died for each other." Just as Ponyboy yearns for the golden Garden of Eden, where all can live the natural, uncomplicated life, so Mark (and later Rusty-James) yearns for the heroic "all for one" time of the gangs, a time that is no more, and a time that—the further it recedes into the past—becomes more and more myth, and less reality. A heroic then, to contrast with a more mundane now.

Brothers.

"He was my best friend and we were like brothers." "Me and Mark were always together." "Mark was my best buddy and I loved him like a brother." Bryon harps on this theme so early and often in the book that we begin to wonder why he doth protest so much. Is it because his faith in this deep friendship is so weak it needs to be constantly restated? There is certainly evidence for this.

There is also much evidence for the closeness that Bryon takes so much trouble to emphasize. There is, for example, the instantaneous communication they share: "Mark followed my train of thought, just like he always had." There are a number of times in the book when Mark almost literally reads Bryon's mind. There are not, on the other hand, all that many instances of the reverse, of Bryon's reading Mark's thoughts. There are instances of Bryon's being judgmental, of his having sudden insights into Mark's suddenly dismal character, but not many where there is evidence of shared insight from his initiative. Unfortunately, this does not seem out of character.

While there are similarities between them there are also marked differences, which are brought forth from the beginning. In some ways these differences can serve to strengthen their devotion to each other; this is a common enough phenomenon. As Bryon says, "I was the hustler and Mark was the thief. We were a great pair." Their differences, then, can be complementary qualities; their talents can be joined to create a newer, broader, more formidable individual: their sum can be greater than its parts. This is indeed the case early on in the book, when their differences—continually stated—seem to make their friendship stronger. Most of the comments are directed toward surface dissimilarities: "I'm a big guy, dark hair and eyes . . . , Mark was small and compact, with strange golden eyes and hair," "Mark . . . couldn't stand sweet stuff . . . I was putting on weight," but then the surface distinctions begin to hint at more crucial changes going on inside, "[I]t seemed like I was growing an inch taller a week—and Mark was staying as slight and slender as ever."

This is the putative theme of the book: Bryon's growing away from Mark. In fact, Bryon has to make sure we get it, so he tells us: "I was changing and he wasn't." This may be true, but there is some question as to whether Bryon's change is for the better or the worse. In any case, it would appear that Bryon's changing also reveals a new Mark. He's suddenly "capable of murder;" he begins to grow away from the "family" of Bryon and his mother; in short, he is definitely headed "east of Eden." Bryon sets himself up, in his newfound "maturity," as the voice of reason, of rationality, as opposed to Mark's reliance upon instinct, feeling. We can't help thinking about those other two brothers, Cain and Abel, but the analogy breaks down when we ask, which one is which? Mark may be "capable of murder," but it is Bryon who is most comfortable with betrayal.

Other Plot Devices

The Use of Myth.

There is an attention to myth and legend in *That Was Then, This Is Now* that is indicative of more to come. It's a small beginning, but it is a technique that will blossom forth in *Rumble Fish* to suggest layers of meaning behind the myth. In the present book it is the story of Androcles and the lion.

Androcles was a Roman slave who, while in hiding from his master, came upon a lion in the cave. The lion was in pain from a thorn in its paw, which Androcles, taking pity on the creature, removed. As the story goes, much later, when Androcles was tossed to the lions for the sport of the good citizens in the Roman arena, the lion who was to have mauled him turned out to be the very same lion from whose paw he had removed the thorn. This lion, recognizing its former benefactor, refused to harm him.

This is a story of loyalty, and of a kind of providential good luck. Fate in this story is a thing with vision. Once again, however, Hinton has intentionally turned this vision on its head. Bryon asks, "What'd I ever do to deserve you, Mark? Pull a thorn outa your paw?" Like the lion of the story, Mark stays loyal. He's a kind of guardian lion for Bryon. In the end, though, this loyalty is rejected, spurned. It's almost as if Androcles, after being spared by the lion, sells him to the circus where he belongs. In *That Was Then, This Is Now* fate is blind. As Mark says, "Things happen, that's all there is to it."

Mike Chambers's long story about the black girl's betrayal serves the same purpose. In a world where fate is this capricious, there is little in the way of fairness to hope for. *Rumble Fish* takes this theme further.

Literary References.

As with *The Outsiders,* there are literary references in this book that serve to expand the book's meaning, but they are fewer, and clearly less important, less revealing than they were in the earlier book. There is the mix-up of Bryon and Lord Byron, which is made by M&M and which Mark doesn't get. There is the more important fact that Mark doesn't read, period. "Mark was too lazy or too uninterested to read himself; he had never bothered to learn how to read very well in the first place." Reading, in *The Outsiders,* usually said something important about the characters, about their level of intelligence and their general interest in the wonders of the world. Ponyboy reads and, in the next book, *Rumble Fish,* the Motorcycle Boy reads, but Rusty-James doesn't. In Mark's case, though, it has nothing to do with either intelligence or interest ("Mark was very quick . . . ," and he was "interested in lots of things—he knew all about the Old West and was nutty about Warner Brothers cartoons"). No, in Mark's case his refusal to read, or even to learn to read properly, is more a conscious choice on his part. It's something Peter Pan would do, to keep from growing up.

Bryon of course reads. He used to do the reading for Mark, when they were little, "books like *Lone Cowboy* by Will James." Lately though, "When I read, I like stuff like Hemingway." This seems a curious revelation, particularly considering the author's stated aversion to Hemingway. "I don't read Hemingway," she said flatly, in an autobiographical sketch written not too long after *That Was Then, This Is Now.*[16] Maybe it's a reflection of Bryon's old, prechange reading habits, but it may also show the author's ambivalence. How sympathetic could she be toward a character who reads Hemingway?

Animal Imagery.

Animal imagery is another characteristic of style that is to have a much more elaborate role to play in *Rumble Fish,* but which makes a small appeareance here. It is evident primarily in the identification of Mark with the lion. Saint Mark the Evangelist is also associated with the lion, but in this case the main association is with the animal itself, and with the variety of responses the lion calls forth. In fact, Hinton uses the many guises of the lion to show the progression and change in Mark (or, more properly, in Bryon's perception of Mark) during the time of the book. Mark is described, progressively, as follows:

13	". . . like a friendly lion."
75	". . . like an innocent lion."
98	". . . suddenly turn on people, like a teased lion . . . ."
113	". . . a pet lion. . . . Golden, dangerous Mark. . . ."
129	"He stayed all night . . . guarding me (like a guardian lion)."
151	". . . stray lion."
157	". . . an impatient, dangerously caged lion."
158	". . . his eyes were like the golden, hard, flat eyes of a jungle animal."

Note the transition from friendly and innocent to impatient, dangerous, and hard. Mark turns from a plaything to a jungle animal. There is a bit of a tendency, perhaps, to beat the metaphor to death, but it seems a chance well taken. There is the same tendency in *Rumble Fish,* and the chance is well taken there, also. Like the use of myth, this extended use of animal metaphor can, when it works, broaden the stage upon which the story plays; it can expand it a little, give it a sense of the timeless.

The Characters

Putting everything else aside for the moment, the book stands or falls on the credibility of the characters. It was the same with *The Outsiders* and, as we saw, that book was successful for that very reason. In particular, we have to be able to put our trust in the voice of the narrator, Bryon Douglas. If, like Charlie, we find we cannot fully trust his voice, there will be problems.

Bryon.

As the narrator, Bryon fits the Hinton tradition pretty well. He's articulate; he gives the impression of self-awareness ("I wanted her to be crazy about me. I'm like that. I have a very bad ego hang up"); his voice has occasional hints of Ponyboy and Rusty-James and, to a lesser extent, Tex, but it's just a little different. It's missing that touch of vulnerability that makes them so real. Whatever vulnerability Bryon might have is hiding behind a mask of bitterness.

His bitterness would be acceptable if it were earned, if he put some kind of innocence on the line and had it taken away from him. The problem is that he doesn't put things on the line. He usually plays it safe. With Cathy, "I decided to play it safe and not kiss her." With Charlie, "with big guys, it's safer to be careful." He doesn't risk anything, usually, so that when he finally risks what ought to be his most important thing, Mark's friendship, we're left feeling—not that he's taken that crucial risk, at last—but rather that perhaps Mark's friendship was not that all-fired important anyway.

His attitudes toward things like class, money, clothes—concerns that were so important in *The Outsiders*—are unremarkable and, at their worst, pedestrian. He's not much interested in the class differences that bugged Ponyboy and Johnny. He's interested in clothes, and how he looks, much more so than his "brother." And then there is his odd obsession with money. Listen to these sentences in which both money and his mother are mentioned (see if it is clear which of the two is more important to him):

> When my old lady went into the hospital, we got so low on money that I bought some clothes there [a secondhand clothing store]. It's pretty lousy, buying used clothes.

> She had just had a big operation, one that cost a lot of money.

> Mom had to stay in bed for a month, so we were really getting hard up for money.

His mother spends half the book coming in and out of the hospital, and yet we never even get an inkling of what's wrong with her. He never thinks about it, apparently. We must question his concern for others. When Mark is first arrested, for car theft, Bryon's reaction is relief that "when Mark was finally caught doing this, he was alone. I could have been booked also." When Mark argues for the group feeling of the gang, Bryon responds with an argument for a more mature outlook: "when you know your own personality . . . you don't need the one the gang makes for you," which leads directly to the next scene, with Mike Chambers in the hospital, where Mark opts to stay with him, to "see if he could cheer Mike up," while Bryon, the voice of maturity, leaves, because "things like that depress me." He does, I guess, know his own personality.

On page eighty-seven, Bryon says, as evidence of his change, that "I had quit thinking only about myself, quit pushing for all I could get." Could that be true? Listen to the "concern" for his friend Mark just four pages later: "Branching off from Mark couldn't affect me so much—I ws all wrapped up in Cathy. He was on his own." What a humanitarian.

Bryon's selfishness, in and of itself, wouldn't necessarily doom the character, not if it leads us somewhere, to some kind of awareness, some kind of revelation. Bryon himself wouldn't even have to reach that level of awareness, so long as someone does. At least the reader should get a sense of the curtain pulled back, of the true nature of something revealed, even if Bryon never reaches that understanding himself.

We don't get that with Bryon, unfortunately, for two reasons: like Charlie, we find we can't entirely believe what he says, and, perhaps as a consequence, we can't believe what he does. The last line of the book is a great tingle line ("I wish I was a kid again . . ."); it's wasted, though, on Bryon Douglas.

Mark.

If Bryon represents reason, maturity, Mark represents instinct, youth. He's more the "natural man" that is celebrated as the traditional American hero. He has all the qualities: he's special (as Bryon says, he was "Mark the lion—Mark, different from other people"); he works by a natural intuition ("Mark never paid any attention to how he dressed . . . but somehow he always dressed right for the occasion"); he even has the physical characteristics that set him apart ("his gold hair and strange gold eyes"). His faults, if we can call them that, are the hero's faults: a little overbearing brashness, a readiness to fight, a tendency to act before thinking, and a penchant for vengeance. But Achilles had these, too. They're traditional heroic baggage. Mark even has a mythical real father, to back up his hereditary claim: "The old lady said he had gold hair and gold eyes like mine and that he won all sorts of prizes at the rodeo."

But the Golden Boy (as Charlie calls him) is not slated to stay gold, not in this book. Ironically, he loses his Peter Pan innocence out of caring for Bryon. "I don't know what's the matter with me," he says to Bryon toward the end of the book. "I never worry about 'what if?' I never did until me and Terry came home and found you lyin' there smashed up. Then I think, 'what if?' and look what happens to me." He finds he has lost the ability to fly. Like the lion in the Androcles story, he arrives ready to pay his debt, and to pay with what, to him, is most valuable, his youth, but the gift is rejected. Instead he's betrayed by his brother, who declines to save him, and then Mark—who is at least as abandoned as Dally Winston—refuses to save himself.

In the end, there aren't any heroes in this book. There is, instead, only frustration that the characters—who ought to have been given the chance to achieve heroism or fail at it—seem to have been prevented from even trying.

The Dishonesty Question.

If Bryon gives any evidence of having achieved some real progress, some real self-awareness, some opening up and making vulnerable of himself, then he has a chance at winning our respect. For his bitterness to affect us, we have to know that it has been earned. And in Bryon's case, since as narrator he speaks to us directly, we have to believe him.

Unfortunately, we don't. He's set up as a liar from the very beginning and, although he keeps telling us he's changing, there is no evidence to support his statements. Lacking such evidence, how can we not say, with Charlie, "Bryon, you're an honest kid in most ways, but you lie like a dog."

Since we can't believe Bryon, we are forced to look for independent evidence, and the independent evidence is not comforting. Mark, his closest friend, who could read his mind, is at a loss to explain his actions. His mother, not the most reliable of witnesses, says that he is "getting even with himself," which has a certain Freudian ring to it, but which begs the question: for what? It's an irrational impulse, but in Bryon's case it may be the only explanation.

As his mother says, Bryon "got even with Mark for Cathy, then you got even with Cathy for Mark." She assigns him the motivation of revenge, ironically enough (since he had earlier, in a fit of maturity, rejected revenge as a motivation). In Mark's case, in the case of a brother he loved, there is no such thing as revenge; in such cases it is called, as it was with Cain and Abel, jealousy, and ultimately, betrayal.

Summary

There is much to admire in *That Was Then, This Is Now;* the discipline of the writing shows the serious side of a growing talent. The expansion of themes and techniques, later used to better effect, give promise that such achievements will be forthcoming. There is the good dialogue and the occasionally striking stylistic touches we had come to expect from the author of *The Outsiders:* the description of Angela, for example, whose "eye makeup [ran] down her face in dark streaks . . . like she was behind bars"; and of Angela, again, who had "the kind of face that would probably be strikingly beautiful even if she shaved her head," which, of course, they later do.

The book is indeed "disturbing," but it also gives the impression of something a little less acceptable, something forced, manipulated. We have no right to expect a repeat of the golden idealism of *The Outsiders,* but we do have a right to expect that the new characters be faithfully drawn, that they achieve their bitterness rather than have it gifted upon them.

There are many thematic similarities between *That Was Then, This Is Now* and *Rumble Fish,* not the least of which is the sub-servience of mortals to the demands of time and fate. This is a classical theme, drawn from Greek tragedy. "You don't know what's comin'," Mark says. "Nobody does." Why is it that Bryon Douglas seems so empty, then, even manipulated, while Rusty-James, equally doomed by events he cannot control, seems heroic and human by comparison? One answer is that Bryon lacks that es-sential element of Greek tragedy, the tragic flaw, that human quirk of personality (whether it be pride or loyalty or whatever) that would allow him to participate in the tragedy. The character of Bryon Douglas has been washed clean of such human quirks, other than perhaps selfishness, so that what is left seems strangely hollow, and the tragedy lacks a human face.

The problem with *That Was Then, This Is Now* is that it is too much like its main character, Bryon Douglas. It has the discipline and strength of character to resist the easy choices, the convenient idealism. But it needs to be more like Mark the guardian lion. It needs to keep the faith. It needs to care more, and reason less. That's what *Rumble Fish* does.

Publicity shot of Hinton with *Rumble Fish*.
Courtesy of the Tulsa Daily World.

4. *Rumble Fish*

"I was hanging out at Benny's, playing pool, when I heard that Biff Wilcox was looking to kill me." With this blunt, almost bored observation begins the short, minimalist, and yet dreamy narrative that is the main story line of *Rumble Fish*.

Framed by the first and last chapters, which take place some time later, the main story line comprises a brief series of events, united by the continuing presence of the Motorcycle Boy, the narrator's brother (though we don't learn even this about him until we are well into the book).

After falling asleep at his girlfriend Patty's, and nearly missing the fight, Rusty-James and his friends from Benny's, including Smokey and B. J. and, later, Steve, meet with Biff Wilcox and some of his friends in the vacant lot between the pet store and the river. Rusty-James and Biff are there to fight; their friends are there to counter one another. Biff is obviously high on pills and this worries Rusty-James somewhat. He becomes much more worried when Biff, wild-eyed, suddenly pulls a knife, but Rusty-James succeeds in knocking the knife away from Biff and then beating him until it would appear the fight has ended. His concentration is broken, though, by the voice of the Motorcycle Boy, "I thought we'd stopped this cowboys and Indians crap." Biff takes this opportunity to grab the knife and stab Rusty-James in the side. The Motorcycle Boy ends it quickly by stepping in and breaking Biff's wrist, "like a matchstick."

Steve and the Motorcycle Boy take Rusty-James home, to an

apartment the two brothers share with their father, and they
patch up the wound in his side. The Motorcycle Boy, who had
earlier been expelled from school for passing in "perfect tests,"
has been out in California and has only just returned. Rusty-
James falls asleep dreaming of his brother and how he, Rusty-
James, will someday be "just like him."

He drags himself to school the next day and to Benny's that
afternoon. Steve's mother has gone into the hospital with a stroke
and Steve is preoccupied, so much so that he fails to pay attention
to Rusty-James as the latter is busy stealing a set of hubcaps
from a nearby car. His attention is captured, though, when three
older guys, one of them presumably the car's owner, come charg-
ing out of a doorway. The boys just barely get away, over some
rooftops, but not without Rusty-James's wound opening again.

As he limps home Rusty-James meets Cassandra, the Motorcycle Boy's "girlfriend," who has begun using heroin. "I thought
he was gone for good," she says. That evening, Rusty-James, the
Motorcycle Boy, and their father talk for a while, but most of it
is over Rusty-James's head. At about midnight Smokey comes by
to get him and they go to the lake. "There were some girls there
and we built a fire and went swimming."

This little party at the beach, which lasts until 5:00 A.M., results
in Rusty-James's both being expelled from school and being ditched
by his girlfriend Patty. Unable to do anything about either of
these events, he feels he has to try to forget about them. To help
him do so, he talks Steve and the Motorcycle Boy into going out
that night, across the bridge to the strip, where everything is
colorful and vibrant. Rusty-James loves it; he loves the color and
noise. He and Steve get a bit tipsy from drinking cherry vodka.
The Motorcycle Boy tells him of having seen their mother in
California. She had abandoned them years ago, when the Motorcycle Boy was six and Rusty-James two. Their father had taken
to drink then (and continued at it; the Motorcycle Boy figures he
took a liking to it) and Rusty-James had been left alone for three
days in an empty house. As the Motorcycle Boy puts it, "I suppose
you developed your fear of being alone then."

Later that night, after watching the Motorcycle Boy in a pool game, Rusty-James and Steve lose track of him and find themselves suddenly alone in a unfamiliar street. They are attacked by two muggers, and Rusty-James is hit in the head with a tire iron. He has about given up hope, assuming they'll both be killed, when the Motorcycle Boy appears from out of nowhere to save them. Once again, Steve and the Motorcycle Boy bring Rusty-James home to recover.

The next day Rusty-James begins to have trouble with his vision and hearing. He gobbles aspirin against the pain and, even more worrisome, he begins to feel a premonition that the Motorcycle Boy is planning something rash. He's been told that the Motorcycle Boy has begun hanging around the pet store looking at the Siamese fighting fish and that he's also being followed by Patterson, the police officer who holds a grudge against him.

Rusty-James watches the Motorcycle Boy at the pet store, while the Motorcycle Boy, fascinated, watches the rumble fish. Would the fish act that way, would they kill each other, if they were in the river? Later that night the Motorcycle Boy goes back to the pet store and sets all the animals free. Rusty-James tries to stop him, but to no avail. The Motorcycle Boy is carrying the rumble fish to the river when suddenly shots ring out and he falls, just at the river bank, the fish flipping and dying beside him. Rusty-James has an overpowering vision of a colorless world, a silent world inside a glass bubble, reminiscent of that in which the Motorcycle Boy lived. He slams his fists through a police car window and they take him away, in a state of shock, to the hospital.

Background

The idea for *Rumble Fish* arose out of a picture of a boy and a motorcycle, published in a national magazine sometime around 1967. Hinton cut the picture out and kept it, carrying it with her, soon forgetting why and even where it had appeared. She still has it, framed, and in fact recently she met someone who, eerily enough, had preserved the very same picture, without knowing precisely why, and showed it to her. The picture, apparently, came from the *Saturday Review*. The coincidence, says Hinton, made her shiver a little. *Rumble Fish,* of course, is, in many ways, about fate.

The book was published in 1975, but the story had been written—in a condensed version—much earlier, well before *That Was Then, This Is Now* was conceived. The short story, "Rumble Fish," was published in the October 1968 edition of *Nimrod,* a special literary supplement to the *University of Tulsa Alumni Magazine.* It was Hinton's only fiction published between *The Outsiders* (April 1967) and *That Was Then, This Is Now* (April 1971).

What is remarkable about the short story is how complete it is, how much it is a fully imagined telling of the tale, in capsule form, that would become the book *Rumble Fish.* All the important scenes are described, including also those events (such as Rusty-James's being left alone for three days, and the Motorcycle Boy's trip to California to see their mother) that occur outside the time of the story. Even the language is familiar. Here are some passages from the story that survive—nearly unchanged, most of them, because the tone is right—to the book:

> . . . the air of a prince-in-exile that the Motorcycle Boy had. . . .

> "Rumble fish," said the Motorcycle Boy, looking at the fish. "They'd kill each other if they could. Wonder if they'd act that way in the river."

> When they turned over he was smiling and the little rumble fish were flipping and dying around him, still too far from the river.

The story, obviously, was fully developed from the beginning. What was missing was the narrator, the point of view. The first point of view in the story is that of the omniscient narrator, the fly on the wall, who watches the Motorcycle Boy with all his eyes, but the point of view then wavers. It slips first to Rusty-James, then to the Motorcycle Boy, and then back to Rusty-James again,

for the ending in the pet store and by the river. This shifting
point of view, not quite convincing, is a symptom of why this
story—otherwise so complete and crying out for expansion to book
length—would be shelved, to be returned to six years later, after
the long writer's block and the therapeutic exercise of *That Was
Then, This Is Now*. It would then be worked and reworked, and
all because of the problem of point of view.

Hinton herself put it this way: "Later, when I decided to do the
novel, I first used Steve as the narrator. . . . I already had the
book done, and I sat and read it over and just couldn't stand it.
It was too easy, he was too intelligent, he was too articulate, too
observant. I had already done several of my narrators like that.
I thought, 'I'm going to tear this up and write it from Rusty-
James' point of view.' That was really difficult, because I'd write
this beautiful sentence and think, 'Ahhh, that's great . . . but
Rusty-James couldn't have said that.' (Makes slashing marks
across an imaginary page) so I'd write some dumb old sentence
in there."[1]

Admirers of *Rumble Fish* are happy for each of those "dumb
old sentences."

Critical Reaction

If the reception accorded *That Was Then, This Is Now* in 1971
was cautiously positive, the reaction to *Rumble Fish* was more
violently mixed. In all the guarded praise that had been passed
out to the earlier books there had been a sense of reservation on
the part of the reviewers. That her books were popular with their
intended readership was undeniable, but the critical jury was still
out on the question of whether that popularity was earned by her
writer's skills or whether it was simply a reflection of her being
in the right place with the right story at the right time.

The Outsiders, after all, could easily be seen as a fluke of the
times: sixteen-year-old author, unimpressed with the books in the
teenage section of her school library, decides to write her own and
the rest is history. This is useful from a public relations stand-

point, but it is not the sort of thing upon which continuing literary reputations are built. *That Was Then, This Is Now* was a bit of a problem. No one really understood it, but no one really tried, either. It was convenient to file it away in the bibliography under DRUGS and let it go at that.

The third book would be the deciding book, at least in the minds of the critics, and with the appearance of *Rumble Fish,* after another four-year wait between books, they had their chance to pass judgment. That judgment was anything but lukewarm.

Publisher's Weekly announced confidently that "Ms. Hinton is a brilliant novelist,"[2] while *Kirkus* observed that Hinton "seems to have no more of a future, or even a present, than Rusty-James has."[3] The two most thoughtful commentaries—one in perhaps this nation's most respected journal of children's literature, the *Horn Book Magazine;* and the other from across the Atlantic, in Margery Fisher's *Growing Point*—could not have been more at odds, though their relative positions were not what one would expect in a review of this thoroughly American writer.

Anita Silvey wrote the piece for the *Horn Book.* Silvey is known for her expertise as a children's book editor, her acumen in the field of children's literature, and her overall generosity toward writing for young adults in particular. One respects, therefore, the sad tone with which her review of *Rumble Fish* ends: "By her third book, the outcome for S. E. Hinton appears to be unpromising; her writing has the same style and the same perception as it had when she was sixteen. Instead of becoming a vehicle for growth and development, the book, unfortunately, simply echoes what came before. She is no longer a teenager writing about teenagers today, and the book raises the question whether, as an adult, she will ever have much of importance to say to young readers."[4]

Meanwhile, Margery Fisher, another respected authority in the field, carries her perfectly British perspective to precisely the opposite conclusion. For her, *Rumble Fish* is "a book as uncompromising in its view of life as it is disciplined in form. Told in flashback, with a carefully placed final chapter, the story has a tight, compact shape within which dialogue and event develop as though with the random order of reality. Of the three striking books by this young author, *Rumble Fish* seems the most carefully structured and the most probing."[5]

What kind of novel is this, to provoke such considered but opposing responses? First of all, *Rumble Fish* is barely a novel at all. It is more a novella, an extended short story, 122 pages comprising fewer than thirty thousand words. All the other Hinton novels are more than half again as long. Far from being the product of haste, however, the brevity of *Rumble Fish* is more the product of control. Its careful construction, and the dreamlike nature of the narrative, would not have worked in a book of traditional novel size.

Unlike the earlier books, with their linear, freight train plots rushing toward defined destinations, *Rumble Fish* seems to meander along. There is action enough, but the plot seems somehow unprovoked, a series of unrelated occurrences submerged within the general mood of the book. *Rumble Fish* is very much a mood piece. It operates on a different level from Hinton's other books, where there may be brief allusions to a larger, more mysterious reality (the implications of the Frost poem in *The Outsiders*, for example), but where the plot is firmly grounded in the actions of the characters and in their clearly defined world. In *Rumble Fish* the world is murky, haunted; it is purposely undefined, and undefinable.

In the film version of the novel (for which Hinton wrote the screenplay) director Francis Coppola was taken to task by critics who claimed he had produced a film overburdened with imagery and suggestion (giant clocks and clouds rushing surrealistically across a plate glass storefront), with not enough substance for film-goers to grasp onto. Like the book, the film seemed to provoke extreme reactions: viewers either loved it or hated it. In fact the film was remarkably faithful to the book, not just in Hinton's dialogue but in the images Coppola chose to capture the mystery, the mythic element that lurks in the novel. The film sought to call up the same emotional charge that the novel conveys, and it succeeds or fails—as does the book itself—by the power of that charge as it is felt in the viewer, or in the reader.

Rumble Fish, Hinton's slightest book, is in fact her most ambitious. The message of the book, the world of the book, is presented by suggestion, in brief scenes of brief phrases. The
inarticulate longing of her narrator makes her earlier heroes seem
almost self-satisfied by comparison. The success or failure of this
book rests with its ability to bring the reader into contact, not so
much with the motivations of the characters or the answers to
their particular problems, but with the mythic element of life
itself, with the element of mystery for which there are no answers
other than belief. For *Rumble Fish* to succeed, one must respond
finally with a tingling at the top of the spine, the body's signal
that it has been in touch with a successful work of art.

Structure and Technique

As she did in *The Outsiders,* Hinton employs a frame to the
story, the main body of which is a series of events that occurred
five years earlier. The story is framed by the first and last chapters, which describe the surprise meeting of Rusty James, the
book's narrator, with Steve Hays, who had been his best friend
during the time the story describes. The story is, in effect, a piece
of Rusty-James's memory, and memory, the ability to remember
things (or, conversely, to forget them) is a concern that appears
throughout the narrative.

There is not much cause and effect in this story. In *The Outsiders* there is a random element to the act of violence that triggers
the story, the stabbing in the park, but once that has occurred,
the rest of the story proceeds with absolute fidelity to the motivations of its characters. Once Johnny stabs Bob, everyone be-
haves exactly as they would be expected to behave, and the story
gathers momentum toward its proper conclusion. In *Rumble Fish*
there is no such turning point, no crucial act or omission (unless
it is the simple returning to town of the Motorcycle Boy) after
which the action of the story becomes inevitable. Instead it is all
random, and it is all inevitable. Like a Greek tragedy dressed in
modern black leather and denim, *Rumble Fish* is the story of

human subservience to fate, to a destiny over which, finally, there can be no control.

We receive all our information in the story through the consciousness of Rusty-James. As with Ponyboy in *The Outsiders* and Bryon in *That Was Then, This Is Now,* this is the narrator's story, filtered through the narrator's point of view. Once again, this technique of first-person narrative permits an immediate involvement on the part of the reader. With Rusty-James we are struck from the beginning by his basic honesty and ingenuousness. "I ain't never been a particularly smart person," he tells us. "But I get along all right." Despite his submission to the macho world in which he lives ("I get mad quick, and I get over it quick"), his voice is a voice whose candor we trust. If we know at times that he is fooling himself we never feel that he is trying to fool us. This adds poignancy to some of his comments about himself, where the war between his outer toughness and his inner sensitivity seems to be proceeding without his notice. "For a tough kid," he says, "I had a bad habit of getting attached to people."

In the early stages of the book, in fact, his teenage braggadocio is both entertaining and revealing:

> I get annoyed when people want to kill me for some stupid little reason. Something big, and I don't mind it so much.

> I'm always in dumb classes. In grade school they start separating dumb people from smart people and it only takes you a couple of years to figure out which one you are.

We can't help but feel that, with an attitude like this, he is not quite so dumb and uncomplicated as he makes himself out to be. As a result we warm up to him further.

In addition to this quality of immediacy, there are two other attributes of the first-person narrative that are of particular importance in *Rumble Fish.* The first is that it must often operate by suggestion. It must somehow transfer to the reader an awareness that is not yet present in the mind of the narrator. Rusty-

James's relationship with his girlfriend Patty is a useful example
of this. She treats him like a yo-yo, leading him on and then
suddenly breaking up with him. Despite this treatment, he continues to believe that they share what he has been told is love.
"I wondered if I loved anybody," he asks himself, and answers,
"Patty, for sure." But in the very same paragraph we read: "Then
I thought of people I could really count on, and couldn't come up
with anybody."

In similar fashion, his preoccupation with appearance, with his
looking like the Motorcycle Boy, or like his mother, and with
sight, vision, builds up throughout the book until it pays cata-
strophic dividends at the end. We can feel it coming, because of
the accumulation of evidence that has made us sensitive to it,
but Rusty-James, whose "loyalty is his only vice," doesn't see it
coming until it runs him down.

It is interesting to note that, since this story is so obviously a
memory, recalled in its entirety in later times, there should be
in the voice of the narrator some indication that he is speaking
from an older, wiser vantage. It is common to stick phrases like
"if I knew then what I know now," or "I couldn't have been more
wrong," at strategic spots, usually near the end of chapters, to
push the story along. Hinton in fact uses this device in *The Outsiders;* at the end of chapter three Ponyboy thinks: "Things gotta
get better, I figured. They couldn't get worse. I was wrong."[6]

In *Rumble Fish* there is a curious absence of this older-but-
wiser voice. The reader accepts this inconsistency without com-
plaint, in part because of the natural complicity of the reader and
the author on behalf of the story, but there is more to it. There
is a clear sense from the beginning chapter that Rusty-James is
still not in complete possession of "the truth" of his story, that
he has instead been running away from it. We get the sense that
he is confronting this story for the first time, that it is as new to
him as it is to us. The immediacy of the first-person narrative
allows us to share the pain and perplexity of his discovery along
with him.

The third quality of first-person narration that is important
here is its ability to capture in the emotion of the narrator the

mood of the times. The sense of confusion, of helplessness in the narrator renders the novel's theme of blind fate and destiny far more effectively than description ever could. As Rusty-James proceeds through the book his voice changes subtly. His apparent arrogance at the beginning ("Pain don't scare me much" on page 29) becomes eroded, and the uncertainty of the murky world he sees around him begins to break through his rather fragile self-confidence. "All my life, all I had to worry about was real things, things you could touch, or punch, or run away from. I had been scared before, but it was always something real to be scared of— not having any money, or some big kid looking to beat you up, or wondering if the Motorcycle Boy was gone for good. I didn't like this being scared of something and not knowing exactly what it was. I couldn't fight it if I didn't know what it was."

At last he discovers that "nothing was like I thought it was . . . everything was changed," but in this he is not entirely correct. In fact nothing has changed, everything is exactly as it was; the only change is his awareness of it, an awareness that had crept into the reader's imagination much earlier, as the tone of the novel shifted ever so gradually from teenage braggadocio to human helplessness.

Because *Rumble Fish* is such an elusive, dreamy book, progress in the story is made by an accretion of awarenesses, a repetition of imagery. It is not so much a question of events turning uncontrollable as it is a growing awareness that events have always been out of the characters' control. The references to time and memory (as instigators of the characters' present lives), to the fleeting color and dreary monotone of life, to insanity and vision, to Greek tragedy and the idea of destiny, all of these gather strength as the novel progresses until the resolution of the story is quite beyond the ability of the characters to change it.

Like the colorful Siamese fighting fish, the Motorcycle Boy, and, to an extent we don't at first realize, his brother, Rusty-James, are trapped by a kind of biological necessity. Victims of their own destiny, of circumstances over which they had no say, their options for the future are very much the classical hero's options. They can, like the Motorcycle Boy, make the Promethean choice—to steal the fire, set free the fish—and suffer the inevitable Promethean punishment of the gods. Or, like Rusty-James, they can try to endure, but this latter choice, to live on in a world stripped of meaning, a world uncolored by hope, is in many ways the more difficult of the two. "I figured if I didn't see [Steve], I'd start forgetting again," Rusty-James says. "But it's been taking me longer than I thought it would."

It may take him the rest of his life.

Imagery and Metaphor

The most striking and persistent image of the book is certainly that of color and monotone, and of vision in general (with all that the word implies). Part of the reason that the movie version offended those of more delicate sensibility was that it took this central metaphor of the book and turned it into a much more visual presence in the film. The film is shot in black-and-white, mimicking the color-blind world of the Motorcycle Boy, with only the fish, bright red and blue, colored individually onto the screen. The result was either blantant exhibitionism (for those who hated the film) or movie magic (for those who loved it).

The contrast between color and monotone is much more subtly handled in the book. The Motorcycle Boy, that model of perfection in the world of *Rumble Fish,* is color-blind. His color blindness is not just a problem with red and green; it is total. The world to him looks like "Black-and-white TV, I guess. . . . That's it." Hinton's decision to bestow upon this larger-than-life figure the curious imperfection of color blindness is, I think, inspired, and it reflects the enchantment of this particular book, as well as the levels of meaning with which it operates in the reader.

Our first reaction to the color blindness is that it sets the Motorcycle Boy apart from the ordinary. It is, after all, a relatively uncommon condition. Furthermore, it is a condition with hereditary connotations, the kind of malady, like hemophilia, that besets royal houses, a condition of imperfection that at the same time suggests a privileged blood line. And of course the question of heredity, of propinquity, is a recurring obsession with this family, and with Rusty-James in particular. He is forever wondering who looks like whom in the family, and who has inherited what from each of their parents. It is of extreme importance to him that he find a permanent spot in the hopelessly dispersed and unresponsive family lineage represented by his absent mother and his functionally absent father.

Rusty-James yearns most of all for a merging with his brother, but the color blindness is a clear and constant reminder of how dissimilar they are. Rusty-James loves color. He loves the colored lights of the city because for him they represent life in all its vibrant potential. He's proud of the uncommon color of his hair, "an odd shade of dark red, like black-cherry pop." In one of his better lines, early in the book, he says, "I like blond girls. I don't care how they get that way."

Color is an important symbol of life for Rusty-James but he would give it up in a minute (just as he would kill to have someone finally say that he resembles his brother) for the more profound message of color blindness. The color blindness of the Motorcycle Boy is a sign that he is one of the Elect, the special ones, and Rusty-James mistakes this sign of exceptionality for the designation he truly seeks, that of belonging. Rusty-James will grasp at straws, and it is only at the end of the book, when in an earth-shattering moment he is allowed to participate in his brother's tragic imperfection, that the bleak reality of the Motorcycle Boy's vision becomes apparent to him.

All of this would have justified Hinton's use of the motif of color blindness and assured it of a central place in the novel. The weight of the metaphor goes deeper, though, and it finally defines the world of *Rumble Fish* as surely as it marks the character of the Motorcycle Boy.

"Sometimes," the Motorcycle Boy says, "it seems to me that I can remember colors, 'way back when I was a little kid. That was a long time ago." This wistful comment suggests that the Motorcycle Boy's color blindness is not a congenital condition at all. It suggests instead that this vision of his is something he's attained, a product of his life. Whether his attainment of this vision is to be considered a gift or a deprivation is not clear. What is clear is that, in *Rumble Fish* at least, the world of light and color that Rusty-James so admires is exposed as an illusion, a child's vision, and the monotone world of the Motorcycle Boy is the reality.

The Motorcycle Boy is the classical hero turned upside down. He's the "perfect knight," the "pagan prince," who sees into the heart of things, "the laughter shining dark out of his eyes." "[The Motorcycle Boy] saw things other people couldn't see, and laughed when nothing was funny. He had strange eyes—they made me think of a two way mirror. Like you could feel somebody on the other side watching you, but the only reflection you saw was your own."

Like Mr. Kurtz in Conrad's *Heart of Darkness,* the Motorcycle Boy has seen too deeply into the secrets of things, into a reality that is gray and desperate. He has seen too much to be able to live a normal life in the world of colored lights and party sounds. In fact, like the tragic hero of that earlier book, he has seen too much to be able to live at all.

The book itself gradually takes on his vision. Things become murky, and motivations blurred. It culminates in Rusty-James's finally getting what he has so devoutly wished for, a merging of his identity with that of his idolized brother, in the penultimate scene by the river. This scene is rendered in such a way that one can only see it as a case of the curtain being suddenly torn open, revealing the brutal reality beneath. "The next thing I knew I was thrown up against a police car and frisked. I stared straight ahead at the flashing light. There was something really wrong with it. I was scared to think about what was wrong with it, but I knew, anyway. It was gray. . . . Everything was black and white and gray. It was as quiet as a graveyard. . . . I was in a glass bubble and everyone else was outside it and I'd be alone like that for the rest of my life."

Hinton's deft handling of imagery and symbol does not confine itself to color and vision. The river, which divides the main part of the city from the boys' neighborhood, becomes a powerful symbol of their life, their world. The Motorcycle Boy stares into the river, as if looking for messages. Rusty-James thinks that the river stinks; he'd just as soon get away from it. The contrast to the river is, of course, the ocean, which the Motorcycle Boy had the chance to see (and didn't) in California and which entrances Rusty-James. "No kidding," he says of the Motorcycle Boy's trip to California. "The ocean and everything" "Kid," the Motorcycle Boy responds, cryptically, "I never got past the river." It is significant that, when the Motorcycle Boy decides to liberate the rumble fish from their glass bowls (recalling the glass bubble in which he lives) he wants to see "if they'd act that way (destroy one another) in the river." His dramatic attempt to release the Siamese fighting fish is an effort not to save them, or even to free them really; it is merely the preparation for the real test, the trial by combat. The Motorcycle Boy is not much interested in their salvation; he is more interested in measuring how their colorful belligerence, their legendary powers of self-destruction perform in the real world, in his monotone world of the river. Ironically, neither he nor the fish are permitted to complete this test. Rusty-James is there to watch. "I was at a dead run at the first shot, and almost to the river by the second. So I was there when they turned him over, and he was smiling, and the little rumble fish were flipping and dying around him, still too far from the river." This is an impressive image, reminiscent of the Viking funeral in *Beau Geste* (the name in French means beautiful, but empty, act), the larger-than-life hero and his totem dying together on the banks of that dark river.

The totemic relationship between the Motorcycle Boy and the rumble fish brings us to one last observation on the sustained imagery of the novel. There is, in *Rumble Fish,* a continued effort to imply animal surrogates for nearly all the main characters. Hinton had done this in other novels (Mark the lion, notably, in *That Was Then, This Is Now*), but there is in no other book the relentless identification of people with specific animals. Early on, Rusty James notes that "the animals reminded me of people. Steve looked like a rabbit. He had . . . a face like a real sincere rabbit." This is a descriptive image, used once, but Hinton does not seem to want us to forget this identification. Steve looks like a rabbit again on the roof after the hubcap escapade and, later, after his mother has gone into the hospital, he "looked like a sincere rabbit about to take on a pack of wolves."

The other characters have their own animal descriptors. The Motorcycle Boy "looked like a panther or something." When Steve shows his displeasure at something the Motorcycle Boy says, he looks like "a rabbit scowling at a panther." The picture of the Motorcycle Boy in the magazine "made him look like a wild animal out of the woods."

The Motorcycle Boy is, fittingly, associated with the panther, exotic and sleek, while Rusty-James is compared most often with a more familiar and domestic creature: a dog. He feels "the hairs of my neck starting to bristle, like a dog's." After he's nearly killed by muggers he makes "a grunt that sounded like a kicked dog." This identification is part of his self-image, and it is revealing to note that, among all the animals he could have chosen, he chooses the common, loyal, unremarkable dog. Even sadder is the animal the Motorcycle Boy assigns to him, the chameleon, which changes its very appearance to suit its environment and thus belongs everywhere, and nowhere.

Besides being graphic and descriptive (who can help picturing Steve as the sincere rabbit or the Motorcycle Boy as the sleek panther?), the association with animals reemphasizes the primacy of fate and destiny in the lives of the characters. What choice does an animal have in being what it is? Hinton's continued introduction of animal references also prefigures the final scene, where the Motorcycle Boy frees all the animals and casts his lot with the rumble fish.

At first glance the rumble fish seem to come out of nowhere. Their existence isn't even mentioned until the very end of the book. How is it that they are suddenly thrust into a position of such crucial importance, prominent enough to give the book its title?

The answer is that their role has been suggested all along, their existence predicted as surely as if Cassandra, the Motorcycle Boy's "girlfriend" (who is associated with cats, the animal symbol of prophecy), had gone into a white-eyed trance and begun raving about them. It wouldn't have mattered anyway, if she had. In

Greek mythology Cassandra is given the gift of prophecy and then punished by Apollo, who ensures that nothing she says, no disaster she correctly predicts, will be believed by anyone who hears her. In *Rumble Fish,* where destiny is forever unalterable, her punishment remains in effect.

The Theme of Destiny and Biological Necessity

There are characters in all the Hinton novels who appear to be victims of a destiny they are not able to escape. This destiny may be the product of an accident of birth or a quirk of society (or a combination of both) but, whatever the cause, it is usually final, and often fatal. Dallas Winston in *The Outsiders* is doomed from the first time we meet him; he can't escape his fate because it is a part of himself. Neither, apparently, can Mark in *That Was Then, This Is Now,* although his case is a little less satisfactory. In her fourth book, *Tex,* the entire cast of characters lines up behind placards reading "Those Who Go and Those Who Stay"; once it's decided which they are (a gypsy fortune teller may make the decision) their fate is sealed.

A similar situation exists in *Rumble Fish.* Rusty-James, whom Steve compares to "a ball in a pinball machine," has given up on his ability to make decisions about his life before the story even begins. Biff Wilcox wants to kill him; Patty wants to break up with him; nothing he can do about it. That's just the way things are. It is instructive to remember just how trivial the so-called causes of these two major rifts are. In the first case he is almost killed as a result of "something [he] said to Anita at school." Who's Anita, anyway? In the second case he loses Patty, someone he professes to love, over an incident at the lake that is of such importance that it occupies one full sentence in the book. Why doesn't he fight back? Why doesn't he even try to make his case with Patty?

He doesn't try because he has come to believe that it won't do any good. Things are what they are, and nothing he can do will change that.

Rusty-James does have aspirations, of course, but they involve magical transformations rather than effort on his part. It is his hope that he will someday be like the Motorcycle Boy, and he bases this hope on heredity. Biology is destiny for Rusty-James, or at least he hopes it is.

> "We look just like each other," I said.
> "Who?"
> "Me an' the Motorcycle Boy."
> "Naw."
> "Yeah, we do."

> The Motorcycle Boy was the coolest person in the whole world. Even if he hadn't been my brother he would have been the coolest person in the whole world.
> And I was going to be just like him.

The irony, unfortunately, is that he succeeds. Biology becomes destiny, although it is necessarily an imperfect copy. Steven makes the connection in the two frame chapters at the beginning and end of the book.

> "Rusty-James . . . you gave me a real scare when I first saw you. I thought I'd flipped out. You know who I thought you were for a second? . . . You know who you look just like?"

> I never thought you would, but you do. You don't sound like him, though. Your voice is completely different. It's a good thing you never went back. You'd probably give half the people in the neighborhood a heart attack."

The Theme of Belonging and of Being Alone

Rusty-James, the tough kid with the bad habit of getting attached to people, is one of Hinton's most ingenuous, most likable creations. He is indeed as loyal as a pet dog, and equally incapable of guile. He can't even play poker because (though he doesn't agree) his friends can read his every emotion in his face. It is therefore all the more tragic when he is transfigured (in an operation only partly successful, like a botched job done by a mad scientist in a horror movie) into the cold, featureless persona of the Motorcycle Boy. All he ever wanted was to belong. Somewhere. Anywhere.

His need for other people, his yearning to belong somewhere, permeates the consciousness of the book. Hinton's characters have always had a bad start at belonging—most of them have dead, absent, or ineffectual parents—but for none of them is the need for a place in life, amongst other people, as strong as it is for Rusty-James. For Rusty-James it is almost a matter of life and death.

> I can't stand being by myself. That is the only thing I am honest-to-God scared of.

> "I don't like bein' by myself. I mean, man, I can't stand it. Makes me feel tight, like I'm being choked all over."

There is an ostensible explanation for this fear. It is given by the Motorcycle Boy, in his sometimes exasperating, emotionless monotone. "When you were two years old, and I was six, Mother decided to leave. She took me with her. The old man went on a three-day drunk when he found out. He's told me that was the first time he ever got drunk. I imagined he liked it. Anyway, he left you alone in the house for those three days. We didn't live where we do now. It was a very large house. . . . I suppose you developed your fear of being alone then."

A two-year-old left in the house alone for three days could develop a great many things, including death. The Motorcycle Boy's explanation is a little too pat, a little too convenient. It was a mistake on Hinton's part to imagine that we needed this kind of traumatic antecedent for the pervasive yearning to belong that exists in Rusty-James's character. The fact of his mother's abandonment of them would have been quite enough; Rusty-James succeeds on his own, in the strength and pure longing of his voice, to convince us of the impact this abandonment has had on him.

The reverse of belonging is, naturally, being alone, and there is no one more alone than the Motorcycle Boy, living in a glass bubble, which Rusty-James inherits at the end of the book. At the risk of being redundant, we must once again mention the irony: Rusty-James, whose very nature is built around the need for people (he makes lists of people he likes, when he's alone, because "it makes me feel good to think of people I like—not so alone") is led by his reverence for the Motorcycle Boy to the precise condition that terrifies him. He is truly and finally alone.

The Theme of the Perfect Knight and the Misfit

Which brings us to the Motorcycle Boy. The first-born son of a morganatic marriage between a mysterious, absent, movie-actress mother and a cerebral, formal, lawyer-turned-drunkard father, the Motorcycle Boy comes stocked with all manner of mythic associations. His name, "like a title or something," his ability to crack Biff Wilcox's wrist "like a matchstick," his inherited imperfection, his profound and eerie effect on everyone he encounters, everything about the Motorcycle Boy is of unearthly stature. When the Motorcycle Boy is expelled from school, Rusty-James wants to know why.

> "How come you got expelled?" I asked.
> "Perfect tests."
> You could always feel the laughter around him, just under the surface, but this time it came to the top and he grinned. It was a flash, like lightning, far off.
> "I handed in perfect semester tests."

Everything about the Motorcycle Boy is preternatural, even his laughter, especially his laughter. "As far as I could tell," Rusty-James says, "he never paid any attention to anything except to laugh at it."

"That cat is a prince, man," says the black pool player during his match with the Motorcycle Boy. "He is royalty in exile." This summation is echoed by the boys' father, in his "perfect knight" speech, recalling the archetypal perfect knight, Sir Galahad in the Holy Grail legend. Galahad is also gifted with uncommon vision, with the ability to see into the secrets of things, "those things that the heart of mortal man cannot conceive nor tongue relate."[7] Like the Motorcycle Boy, the character of Sir Galahad is often perceived to be "a cardboard saint, [whose] austere virtue excludes humanity."[8] Galahad succeeds in his quest for the Holy Grail—only a perfect knight can accomplish this—but the Motorcycle Boy's quest is directionless, his goal unidentified, and whether his smile at the end is an indication of the success or the failure of his private quest is open to debate.

The implications, for both the Motorcycle Boy and Rusty-James, of their father's "perfect knight" speech are worth considering. "Russell-James," the father says, "every now and then a person comes along who has a different view of the world than does the usual person. . . . [The Motorcycle Boy] is merely miscast in a play. He would have made a perfect knight, in a different century, or a very good pagan prince in a time of heroes. He was born in the wrong era, on the wrong side of the river, with the ability to do anything and finding nothing he wants to do."

After this speech, Rusty-James says, in his wide-eyed, great-hearted innocence, once again, "I think I'm gonna look just like him when I get older. Whaddya think?" His father is shocked by this pronouncement, and looks at him as if seeing him for the first time. What he sees startles him, and then reduces him to pity. "You poor child," he says. "You poor baby."

The flip side of the perfect knight is the misfit. Their father's "perfect knight" speech could just as easily be called his "misfit" speech, and it applies to Rusty-James as well. He, too, is miscast in the play, born in the wrong era. He, too, is out of touch with the times, though his options are fewer and his "time of heroes" is more recent. With typical misunderstanding, Rusty-James locates this heroic time with the era of the gangs, just recently passed, which he imagines would have provided him with meaning, belonging. He even romanticizes that time out of its own chronology; for him the heroic era was "a long time ago, when there were gangs."

His misapprehension of the reality of the gang era doesn't make him any less the misfit in the present time. The lot of the misfit is never a pleasant one. In Flannery O'Connor's short story "A Good Man is Hard to Find" there is a chilling, murderous character known only as The Misfit. There is nothing particularly heroic about The Misfit; the only startling thing about him is the utter amorality and the cold expressionlessness with which he goes about the business of murdering, one by one, the members of a family whose car has broken down. At the end of the story, The Misfit engages the grandmother of the family in an extended, almost overrational explanation of why he lives as he does in a world where the possibility of redemption, of meaning, is so uncertain. The grandmother, who is doddering in and out of reality, mistakes him in a visionary moment for one of her children and she reaches out to touch him. He recoils in horror and kills her. The last words of the story, spoken in a final attempt at self-justification by The Misfit, are "It's no real pleasure in life"[9]

The Motorcycle Boy couldn't have said it any better.

The Problem of the Motorcycle Boy

Steve says of the Motorcycle Boy, "[H]e is the only person I have ever met who is like somebody out of a book. To look like that, and be good at everything, and all that." Thus does one of the book's characters state the main problem about the Motorcycle Boy. People in books should not themselves appear to come out of books; that's too much of a jump for any character to make, and the Motorcycle Boy, who doesn't make the river at the book's end, doesn't make the jump into fully realized existence either. He's just too distant, too idealized, too detached, and finally too inhuman to be taken seriously as a character. Robert Berkvist, in his otherwise not very probing review of *Rumble Fish* in the *New York Times Book Review*, makes the entirely accurate observation that the Motorcycle Boy "clanks through the story like a symbol never quite made flesh."[10]

If Hinton thought to introduce some humanity into the character by means of the color blindness (and it is not my belief that she did), the result is quite the opposite. His color blindness, along with his occasional deafness and his general otherworldliness, only serve to set him off further from the rest of humanity. His detachment is so total that he ignores the person closest to him, the person who truly cares about him, his brother, Rusty-James.

Numerous times in the novel Rusty-James makes statements like "one of the few times he ever paid any attention to me," "he never paid much attention to me," "in case the Motorcycle Boy forgot I was with him," and "the Motorcycle Boy was watching me, amused but not interested." The key is that, with the depth of feeling the reader has built up around the character of Rusty-James, we should hate this Motorcycle Boy character for the way he treats his hero-struck younger brother. In fact, though, we don't feel much about the Motorcycle Boy, pro or con. We don't feel much because he's not real; it would be like trying to raise an emotion about a lounge chair or a suitcase.

There is the matter of his speech, for one thing. How are we to deal with a character who talks like this? "It's a bit of a burden to be Robin Hood, Jesse James and the Pied Piper. I'd just as soon stay a neighborhood novelty, if it's all the same to you. It's not that I couldn't handle a larger scale, I just plain don't want to."

Hinton tries to have Rusty-James explain this away by saying, "Sometimes, usually on the streets, he talked normal. Then sometimes he'd go on like he was reading out of a book, using words and sentences nobody ever used when they were just talking." This just doesn't wash; it's too unreal. The only useful purpose to this kind of speech is that it makes the heredity case once again; it links the Motorcycle Boy with his father, who talks the same way. Compare the father's quizzical "What strange lives you two lead" with the Motorcycle Boy's "What a funny situation . . . I wonder what I'm doing here," after Rusty-James is injured in the mugging scene. (A few pages earlier, when Rusty-James thought he was dying, he thinks, "I pictured my father at my funeral saying, 'What a strange way to die.' " Rusty-James has a talent for capturing the essence of character.)

In Hinton's defense, the problem she bit off when she chose to create the Motorcycle Boy is a problem that not many authors have solved well. The problem of the Motorcycle Boy is the problem of trying to create a larger-than-life character—the saint, the seer, the mystic—and at the same time have that character animated by the common spark of humanity we all recognize. Not many writers are able to pull this off. An example of one who tried mightily (and ultimately failed) in recent American writing is J. D. Salinger, with Seymour Glass (another idolized older brother). Seymour Glass, who appears in a number of Salinger's books, finally becomes such a prisoner of his spiritual detachment and doomed purity that the reader can't wait for him to do himself in and get it over with. Like Sir Galahad (or David Bowie's Major Tom), Seymour ascends so far into the stratosphere that it becomes clear that he is never coming back down.

Ordinarily this should prove fatal to a novel, a major character who fails to break through two dimensions into at least the suggestion of a rounded existence, but not so in *Rumble Fish*. *Rumble Fish* succeeds in spite of the Motorcycle Boy because *Rumble Fish* is not the Motorcycle Boy's story at all (despite Hinton's comment that "the Motorcycle Boy haunted me" and that he was the reason she forced herself to come back to the book, after it had been put aside for so long). It's Rusty-James's story, actually, and from the point of view of the reader's allegiance, it is the Motorcycle Boy who plays squire to Rusty-James's knight, and not the other way around.

We can forgive the clanking of the Motorcycle Boy because our attention is focused on Rusty-James. The spark of humanity that is missing in the Motorcycle Boy is a roaring fire in Rusty-James, and it is our concern with this conflagration that gives the book its impact. We imagine that the main thrust of the story is about the Motorcycle Boy, but in this we are fooled (intellectually, not emtionally) by a sleight of hand. As we have seen, upon closer inspection, all the themes of the book, even those having to do with perfection and perfect knighthood, are concerns of the char-

acter of Rusty-James as well as the Motorcycle Boy. If we sometimes cringe at the behavior of the Motorcycle Boy, we never look
away, because in fact it is never the Motorcycle Boy we are truly
looking at. What we are looking at is a distorted mirror, "a distorted glass" reflection of Rusty-James.

In the end we respond to *Rumble Fish* in a much deeper way
than we do to *That Was Then, This Is Now*. It's an emotional,
almost a physical response, as opposed to the more rational, intellectual reaction that the other book prompted. Whatever its
defects, whatever its ambitions only partly achieved, *Rumble Fish*
works as a novel. In its appeal to the mythic element in life, in
its living, breathing creation of the pilgrim character of Rusty-
James, the book works. And there is a name usually given to this
kind of success. It is called art.

Hinton with actor Matt Dillon on the set of *Tex*, 1982.
Courtesy of the Boston Herald.

5. *Tex:* Those Who Go and Those Who Stay

—I had hoped, said Pangloss, to
reason a while with you concerning
effects and causes, the best of possible
worlds, the origins of evil, the nature
of the soul, and pre-established
harmony. . . .

— That is very well put, said
Candide, but we must cultivate our
garden.

Voltaire, *Candide* (1759)

Tex was published in October of 1979, maintaining the four-year interval between publication of each of the four books (a skein broken only when the year 1983 produced a rather different contribution to the Hinton opus: her son Nick).

Despite the stock Hinton answer to the question "Why do you write?" ("The gas bill can be pretty inspiring"), financial success was by this time assured and was not a major consideration. There were well over seven million copies of her first three books in print, and if she were in danger of anything it was not that the gas would be shut off. The real danger, probably, was that she had become, in the world of young adult fiction, something of an institution, a thirty-one-year-old grande dame. A dubious distinction in a field so young.

Patricia J. Campbell, in her monthly column for *Wilson Library Bulletin,* "The Young Adult Perplex," wrote in the October 1979 issue that the "big guns of October have been trundled out," referring to new publications by a number of well-known YA authors, and began with her appraisal of *Tex.* "First, a volley from the heavy artillery. S. E. Hinton is the biggest of the YA big guns."[1] Grande dame or big gun, by this time, twelve years and three books after *The Outsiders,* there was no more formidable reputation in the world of young adult writing than that of S. E. Hinton.

The initial response to *Tex* took this into account. Most of the reviews were politely affirmative. The disagreement and polarizing that had greeted *Rumble Fish* were not appropriate here, so that even *Kirkus Reviews,* which had earlier been rather a disbeliever in the S. E. Hinton way of telling things, had polite things to say about *Tex.* The only jarring notes were reviews in the *New York Times Book Review,* which resurrected the old charges of melodrama and ultrarealism, and a tirade in the London-based *Times Literary Supplement* that ranted on about "machismo," "hairs on the chest of the teenage hero," "male chauvinist piggery," and various other offenses against the reviewer's sensibilities.[2]

Marilyn Kaye's starred review in *School Library Journal* began by drawing attention immediately to the novel's technical prowess: "Hinton's style has matured since she exploded onto the YA scene in 1967 with *The Outsiders.*"[3] Kaye devoted much of the relatively brief review to considerations of story line and plot, character development and theme, and to the novel's preoccupation with "questions about responsibility, friendship, desire, and communication." Conspicuous by its absence was any mention of whether the novel will be popular or not. This comes— after years of reviews ending "should be popular with reluctant readers aged 14–16"—as welcome relief.

Margery Fisher, who had earlier written one of the more perceptive reviews of *Rumble Fish,* did a "Special Review" of *Tex* on the first page of her May 1980 issue of *Growing Point*. Like the *Rumble Fish* review, her appraisal of *Tex* is distinguished by its thoughtful attention to the book's serious nature, to the author's purpose and style, and to the development and expansion of characters. It is not necessary to agree with all of her judgments or conclusions in order to respect her seriousness of purpose, and there are points in her review that are certainly arguable, to say the least. When she is right she is often right on the money, as in her reference to Tex's "unexpected contentment," a phrase that zeroes in on something that is special about Tex and expresses it nicely in two words. Her conclusion is that "in this new book Susan Hinton has achieved that illusion of reality which any fiction writer aspires to and which few ever completely achieve."[4]

Like the earlier books, *Tex* is a first-person narrator's book. It begins with Tex McCormick riding his horse, Negrito, whom he treats more like a friend than an animal, chiding him about his imaginary bears and fear of rabbits. Later, Tex rides to school and back with his friend Johnny Collins, on the back of Johnny's dirt bike, but when he returns home he discovers something odd: his older brother, Mason, who normally devotes his afternoons to basketball, is home. Mason is in his last year of high school, a basketball star with his eye on a good college, and because their father, Pop McCormick, is so often on the road with the rodeo, it is Mason who is in charge of the family. Because Pop has neglected to send money (they haven't heard from him in four months), Mason has had to sell their horses to pay the bills. When Tex hears this he loses control, begins throwing things. Mace wrestles him to the kitchen floor and literally has to beat him into submission.

Tex decides that he's going to find Negrito and get him back. Since Mace won't tell him where the horse is, Tex decides he'll just set off walking until he finds him. Johnny Collins and his sister Jamie come by on Johnny's cycle while Tex is walking, and they try to talk him out of it, but he's too stubborn to listen. Finally Mace comes with the pickup and drags him home.

On Sunday the special yearly fair begins, held in the city, and

Bob, Johnny's older brother, drives Tex and Johnny in. (Mace, who says he's too old for the fair, stays home.) After a few pranks, the two friends meet up with Johnny's sister Jamie and her friend Marcie, who talk them into going to see the fortune teller. The fortune teller tells Tex that "there are people who go, people who stay. You will stay." She also says that he is a "fourth-generation cowboy," which, from all Tex knows, is a couple of generations more than he expected.

Tex and Johnny manage to get into almost continuous trouble, much to the consternation of Cole Collins, Johnny's father, who considers Tex a bad influence. When Lem Peters, one of Mason's old friends, comes back from the city to announce the birth of his son, Jamie draws the ire of all the boys around her by making sarcastic comments about Lem's ability to bring up a child. Only Tex stands up for her (although Mace later agrees) and it is now very clear that Tex's feelings toward Jamie are something more than casual.

Mason and Tex drive into the city, so that Mace can have some tests done at the hospital. The tests show that he has an ulcer. While they are in the city they visit Lem and discover that he is dealing drugs to support his new family and his new city-style life, which he does not wear comfortably. Mace lets Tex drive the pickup back home and, in part to draw Mason's attention away from both Lem and the ulcer, Tex stops to pick up a hitchhiker.

The hitchhiker turns out to be dangerous. He pulls a gun and holds it on Mason. Back in the city, he says, he's shot someone, "a big revenge trip." When Tex notices a state police car following, he spins the truck into a ditch. The hitchhiker attempts to pull Mace out with him, to use him as a shield, but Tex won't let him. At last the hitchhiker lets go, and is killed by the police in a hail of gunfire.

As as result of this, Tex and Mace are shown on newscasts throughout the area, as far away as Dallas, where Pop sees them and calls, telling them he'll be home in the morning. Mason is less than thrilled by this, but Tex is ecstatic. When Pop arrives he and Mace almost immediately get into an argument, but Tex plays peacemaker. Pop, who has forgotten Tex's birthday, promises to get him his horse back at the end of the month. Alas, he forgets about this, also, and when Mace and Tex finally do go for the horse the new owners don't want to sell. For Tex this is like losing Negrito a second time.

Tex and Johnny get into further trouble (as the relationship between Tex and Jamie staggers and stumbles a bit), the worst of it being caught sticking caps on the typewriter keys at school, causing a major commotion in typing class. Cole Collins comes and drags Johnny out, but Tex is forced to wait until four o'clock for Pop. When Pop arrives he and Mace get into another argument, during the course of which Mason says of Tex, "He is my brother even if he isn't your son!" When Pop doesn't deny this, Tex leaves the building in shock, trying to make some sense of it all.

Lem is outside and Tex goes with him, off on one of his drug runs. Lem is glad to have the support—his customers are unhappy customers–and Tex doesn't care. Lem's two customers turn out to be unstable. They panic and one of them takes a shot at Tex with a .22 handgun. Tex wrestles the gun away from him and points it at him; he is prepared to pull the trigger, but at the last moment, thinking of funerals and relatives who grieve for the dead, he doesn't. As he and Lem leave the building he discovers he's been shot. After a lot of confusion Lem, apparently, gets him to the hospital.

Tex is in and out of consciousness at the hospital. Mason and Pop visit. Pop, with some discomfort, tells him the story of his real father, a blond-haired rodeo cowboy. Johnny and Jamie visit. From Jamie he gets a kiss but, of course, no promises. It turns out, also, that it was Cole who had called the ambulance that saved Tex's life.

As Tex recovers, into the spring, Mace announces that he's decided that he won't go to college after all. Tex won't hear of it. "You don't go to college because of me, and in two years you'll hate my guts." Tex compares himself to Smoky the Cowhorse, the title character of his favorite book. "I've been bashed up pretty good, Mason, but I'm going to make it." He has a job lined up, working with horses at the Kencaide ranch. There are people who go and people who stay. . . . Mason should go; Tex will stay.

The Style Matures

There was close to universal agreement among the reviewers on the new "mature" style of *Tex,* usually the result of comparison with the youthful exuberance of *The Outsiders* or with the more personal, more demanding *Rumble Fish.* There will always be strong individual arguments for readers who prefer the unalloyed intensity of *The Outsiders* or the spine-tingling mythmaking of *Rumble Fish,* but there is little doubt that, as an example of mature, polished storytelling, *Tex* is Hinton's most successful effort. All the discipline and control she had to force into *That Was Then, This Is Now* is here brought effortlessly to bear. *Tex* doesn't take the chances that *Rumble Fish* took, but it knows what chances it is willing to take and how to handle them.

In fact *Tex* is clearly the most seamless of her books. The voice is consistent and appropriate throughout. It is Tex's voice, Tex's consciousness. The controlling, manipulating hand of the author is far in the background. For us, the readers, it has disappeared.

This is a style of writing that puts the welfare of the book, and the integrity of the book's voice, above its own need to show off. The most successful fiction—that which will last beyond one day in the sun—always seems to work its magic upon the reader in concealment, lying in wait like an enemy agent, familiar and friendly and certainly unsuspected, until at some point it explodes into an awareness that is truly subversive, that shakes the foundations of the reader's version of comfortable reality. *Tex's* subversion is a modest one, as befits a book of such "unexpected contentment," but in its own way, in the conclusions it draws, the world view that gradually comes into focus behind its exceptional main character, it is as meaningful, and as important, as the shattering monochrome vision of *Rumble Fish.*

Structure

The structure of the book resembles that of the conventional novel much more than anything we've seen before. There are no tricks, no frame chapters or flashbacks. Hinton shows the same restraint with regard to her structure as she has with her style. The approach is straightforward, without embellishment, without anything that might distract the reader from the important matter at hand: the story, as conveyed through the continuing, sure voice of the narrator.

The story rolls along in real time, event upon event, so as to achieve a kind of momentum, a not-to-be-averted quality that reminds us of the carnival gypsy: "There are people who go, people who stay. You will stay." There is no intervention by a more knowing narrator, with access to the future, no one to tease us with hints of secrets he knows and we will only later find out. Tex knows no more than we do about his future. He knows only what he's been told by gypsies and what he's inferred from meetings with hitchhikers and drug dealers, which isn't much. Tex's is a future without the kind of guarantees an omniscient narrator provides. It's the kind of future that needs to be lived in order to see what will happen.

The structure of the novel emphasizes the flow of events. It is the opposite of the staccato structure of *Rumble Fish,* whose technique emphasizes the here-and-now (and the timeless), rather than the gradual flow of time. Chapters in the earlier books are shorter and tend to concentrate on one scene, with the result that—though there are some powerfully rendered scenes—the overall effect is episodic. The action in the earlier books tends to move in an almost cinematic fashion, from scene to scene, with the mood and flow of the story building up out of an accumulation of episodes. There is nothing wrong with this technique, and when it works it works very well, but the structure of *Tex* is the more traditional (let's say, literary, rather than the cinematic) way to do it.

The structure of the book is, finally, in keeping with the *ars est celare artem* (true art conceals art) approach of its style. Understated, conventional, it defers at all times to the story line, to character and plot.

Plot

The plot, outlined earlier, is certainly not lacking in action scenes. Why is it then that we don't emerge from the book with the sense of having read an action/adventure story, as we certainly might have with *The Outsiders,* and even with the other books? Part of it has to do with the more controlled, more confident writer Hinton has become. The action scenes, while still vividly written, are more integrated into the flow of the story line. The impulse of the younger writer might have been to make sure that her action scenes packed a wallop—something she knew she could achieve—to compensate for what she might have felt were inadequacies in other areas. By the time of *Tex* she seems to have become more comfortable with her talent, and those inadequacies, real or imagined, no longer hold much sway on her.

The result is, once again, a more organic, integrated novel. Nothing stands out; nothing detracts from the movement of the book as a whole. Even the central scene with the hitchhiker— major melodrama on the face of it: it could easily have been made as obvious a turning point as the church fire in *The Outsiders*— is quickly disarmed by the horseplay of the television/local hero scenes and by the new turning point (or so we think) of the return of Pop. It is rather surprising, in fact, to note that the hitchhiker, as we shall see, is a rather important figure in the book, so quickly does he come and go.

Another point to consider is that events and scenes don't make it into S. E. Hinton novels as a result of serendipity. Certainly not since *The Outsiders* anyway. All the novels since then have been very clearly worked over, shaped and controlled by the author. Hinton's method of plot construction is a painstaking process, based—as it has been from the beginning—on character, on the reactions of characters to incidents, and to the more subtle structural weave that surrounds them. This is not something that comes without effort.

Her comments in the interview published in the 1983–84 *University of Tulsa Annual* are instructive as to both her methods and her goals.

> I have a real hard time plotting things anyway. And I always have an end in mind. The beginning is kind of easy because you can put characters in any situation. Getting from point A to Z is just so hard for me, and I get off on tangents and write 50 pages on a minor character. So I think, this isn't going in the direction I thought, and I tear it up. What's going to happen next? I need to get "Tex" from there over here, but how do I do that? Sometimes I put it away for months at a time.[5]

Behind her usual self-deprecating tone (the same voice that says the gas bill is an inspiration) there are clues to the close attention paid to the requirements of fitting plot with character: the false starts and wrong turns, the clear direction of the book from its inception, and the occasional frustration when the fit between character and event is wrong ("Sometimes . . . months at a time").

Hinton is, as she has said from the start, a "character writer." "I always start off with characters, and I have to know my characters real well. . . . It doesn't matter if that shows up in the book or not, I have to know them." When you know your characters real well, when you know "what they eat for breakfast, what their sign is," then you will not sacrifice them to the poor fit of an overblown crisis scene. No, their actions and reactions must be true to themselves, or there is no reason to write the book at all.

Character

"I like to think my books show character growth in some way, that the character is always different in the end than he was in

the beginning."[6] ACTION IS CHARACTER, we will recall, was Fitzgerald's uppercase imperative to himself in the notebooks for *The
Last Tycoon*. We have applied this prescription to *The Outsiders*
and seen where the book met—and failed to meet—its requirements. With *Tex* it must be introduced once again because, while
the character of the first-person narrator, and character in general, is important in all the books, in *Tex* it is truly sine qua non,
that without which there is no book. And the character is, of
course, Tex.

We are inside Tex's head and with his thoughts from the first
line. Once inside his head we never leave; we're coaxed into be-
lieving in that voice from the start, and the voice never falters,
so our belief remains strong. It's clear that just one "clanger," just
one miscalculation of what the character might do or say in a
given situation, can destroy the illusion of reality and the reader's
complicity in making that illusion seem real. Many's the novel
that one such foolish move has reduced from the miraculous to
the merely good. *Tex,* whether it be miraculous or not, at least
makes no foolish moves.

S. E. Hinton knows Tex, intimately. She knows how he thinks
and, like a good actor drawing on the experience of her own emotion to animate a character, how he feels.[7] Consequently, the voice
does not seem contrived; it is a true voice.

Other than Ponyboy (whom Hinton admits is perhaps the closest to being an extension of herself, her own voice at the time),
she has never taken the easy way out with her narrators. Bryon
Douglas was an intellectual jigsaw puzzle, a snapshot of bitterness, or betrayal, or self-reliance, or . . . but the pieces never
could be made to fit. Rusty-James, whom Hinton has termed "my
biggest challenge as a writer,[8] emerged out of an inarticulate haze
to steal the book away from his "perfect" brother. Now Tex, neither as bright and analytical as Bryon nor as emotion-driven and
vulnerable as Rusty-James, comes to us with his "unexpected
contentment."

There is a flip side to the requirement that successful characters
be always true to themselves, always "in character," and that is
that they not be boring, that they be, in some sense, unpredictable,

unexpected. Dallas Winston was unpredictable in this sense, as was, because innocence is always unexpected, Rusty-James. Thus, when Margery Fisher uses the word unexpected to describe Tex in the phrase above, she renders him a distinct compliment.

What about the second part of her compliment, the "contentment" part? What is contentment, anyway? Fisher goes on to define it more expansively as "his cheeerful approach to life as it is and not as he would like it to be," which is close, but doesn't quite explain it. Tex's approach to life-as-it-is when life-as-it-is happens to include the sale of his horse hardly qualifies as cheerful. No, Tex is too complicated and real a character to be reduced simply to "cheerful," nor is he always content, satisfied with things as they are, particularly in the early parts of the book. Contentment is an appropriate word, though; it describes something special about Tex, something that distinguishes him from the other Hinton narrators. What it describes, however, is not some quality he possesses in abundance, something he brings to all his human interactions like the wisdom of Solomon, but rather a state of being he achieves, by the end of the book, with the considerable help of other qualities that he does possess in abundance.

Included among Tex's better qualities is his honesty. We believe everything Tex tells us (as opposed to Bryon Douglas, for example, or even Ponyboy) because we believe that he would no sooner lie to us than he would to himself. What Tex knows about himself he will not conceal from us, or from himself. This sometimes means revealing things that are unpleasant. After he tells Mace that he will hate him for the rest of his life, he sees a muscle in his brother's face jump, "and I knew I'd hurt him. It felt good. It was the first time I realized hurting somebody could feel really good."

Tex's honesty (or maybe his inability to be dishonest) makes for a tricky kind of relationship with "the truth." For Mason, truth is "a present I always wanted," but it is a gift for him because it is something he can use. Tex does not have that luxury. For Tex, who cannot compromise his honesty, truth is often better left unknown. Once known, it cannot be ignored or used as he sees fit. Tex won't turn away from unpleasant truths. This is what he tries to explain to Mason in a scene after the shoot-out in which the hitchhiker was killed.

> "Texas," [Mason] said, "why did you have to go look, after they'd killed him? It wasn't exactly a side show at the Fair."
> I was shocked that he could think such a thing. What kind of a creep did he think I was, anyway?
> "I had to," I said finally. "Mason, I killed that guy, as sure as if I'd pulled the trigger. I knew it when I ditched the truck. I couldn't just walk off like nothing had happened. I had to face what I did."

This is a rare kind of integrity in a character, a rare sense of responsibility.

Even more rare—in a character of any age but surely in one so young and presumably self-involved—is the kind of generosity Tex shows toward those around him. It is this generosity of spirit, which he exhibits throughout the book, that paves the way for his unexpected contentment at the end. Not that he's perfect, or ego-less, or free from any taint of spite. He wouldn't be human if he were. But that's what makes so continuously suprising his naturally generous character, his impulse to think the best of people, to give them their best possible lives and to let them diminish those lives, if they must, themselves.

He looks into oncoming cars on the highway and sees, not featureless, strange faces, but people with stories, stories that are "just as important to them as our stuff is to us." "Miss Johnson"— the vice principal—"might swat me once in a while, but she always asked me how we were getting along, if we'd heard from Pop," and made other such overtures that, for Tex, were enough to show that she cared whether he lived or died. "If you get the feeling somebody cares about what happens to you, then you don't mind if they swat you once in a while." Johnny Cade, who had to endure the latter without ever feeling the former, would have agreed.

Miss Johnson's asking about Pop brings up another good case, because Tex's generosity extends particularly to him, especially because Pop does practically nothing to earn it. He forgets Tex's birthday. He shows his obvious preference for Mason, who doesn't even "much like being named after Pop," over and over again. He goes to a pool game in Broken Arrow rather than helping to get Negrito back as he had promised he would do (this last an insensitivity that even the movie version of *Tex* apparently could not stomach; Pop goes with Tex and Mace to try and get the horse back in the movie). Still, at the end of it all, Tex forgives him, the way a patient, loving parent forgives a wayward child. It's not Pop's fault if he forgets. As Tex notes, "He doesn't have a very long attention span."

He is also generous toward the hitchhiker. He needs to explain, if not to justify, the fact of his existence. "Mace, something really bad must have happened to that guy." But his motivation for generosity toward the hitchhiker is a bit more complicated than that which prompts his generosity as a rule; we will look more closely at this later.

Tex is also a creature of hope. Hope is a conclusion that is perhaps impossible for the generous spirit to avoid. It is the conclusion of Smoky the Cowhorse, that sometimes bad things happen they can nearly take the heart out of you—but if you hang on you will see that, like Tex in his time of troubles, "in the morning I'd still be alive, and sometimes the pain seemed a fraction less." This is a definition of hope, to expect that day by day you will awaken and the pain will seem "a fraction less."

Tex also has more conventional hopes, like the poignant "Mason would be gone for college pretty soon and then Pop would have to notice me a little more. I mean, I'd be the only kid, then," but the hope that animates the book is Smoky's hope. "I've been bashed up pretty good, Mason, but I'm going to make it." And we have no doubt that he will.

All these qualities give Tex a kind of innocence, an attitude he shares with characters like Johnny and Ponyboy and Rusty-James, characters who are, at least on the surface, as far from innocent as a street kid can get. There are, of course, two ways of defining innocence: (1) freedom from sin, guilt, imperfection, etc. and (2) freedom from *knowledge* of sin, guilt, imperfection, etc. In this world, since the Fall, there is no innocence in the first sense. There is only innocence within terms of the second definition, and for Hinton characters this innocence is usually under attack, if by nothing else then always by the eroding effects of time in a world of unfriendly truths. Mason's "present I always wanted," truth, is, like Eve's apple, a gift of uncertain value.

Tex's innocence is particularly vulnerable because of his unwillingness to compromise his honesty. He manages to hold onto his enduring innocence, despite all the assaults made upon it, because it is important to his generous view of life. Mason puts it this way, when Tex refuses to feel anything but happiness for Lem and his new baby: "Tex, you are not stupid, and you're not all that ignorant. But how anybody as simple-minded as you are has managed to survive for fourteen years is beyond me." Tex answers back quickly, revealing the temporary, fragile nature of the simple-mindedness (innocence) that Mason deplores: " 'Well, I had a wonderful smart sweet brother lookin' out for me,' I said. I'm not sarcastic by nature, but I reckon you can learn anything if you're around it long enough." The fruit of the Tree of Knowledge includes sarcasm, and much worse.

The theme of innocence, of staying gold, arises in *Tex* nearly unchanged from its statement in *The Outsiders* (and its counterstatement in *That Was Then, This Is Now*). As long as Tex stays "simple-minded," as long as he stays a kid, he stays gold. "I ain't going to outgrow [the fair]," he says to Mace. "I'll think the Fair is fun no matter how old I get." It's Peter Pan again, but Peter's solution, as we saw in *The Outsiders,* is incompatible with life in the real world. One cannot stay gold and stay around. Tex, who is from the beginning one who will stay around and knows it, must make another, more realistic solution. This is where *Tex* takes over and expands upon *The Outsiders*. This is where *Tex* is, in many ways, the summation statement of the unresolved concerns of all three earlier books.

Tex is a character study, and it is an action novel, but at its core it is also a novel of ideas. Not surprisingly, the ideas the novel feels impelled to grapple with are those we have seen before, the troubling, unresolved problems of *The Outsiders, That Was*

Then, This Is Now, and to some extent *Rumble Fish.* And *Tex* the novel is like Tex the character; it wants to find solutions to these problems; it wants to make a working arrangement that will let them all live in the real world. To do so it must deal directly with problems of the real world that have left earlier characters bitter, or puzzled, or just numb.

The Dreams of Orphans and Belonging

> ". . . who was that Connie's always
> saying you look like? Goofy, or—"
> "Bambi."
>
> —*Tex*

Tex is another orphan, another one of the lost boys we first met in *The Outsiders.* All the lost boys want parents; they want to recapture their lost lineage, and Tex is no exception. He wants to belong, as Rusty-James, who makes lists of people he likes, wants to belong. Or as Johnny Cade, who is adopted by the gang only to find it is not enough, wants to belong. Or even Mark, in *That Was Then, This Is Now,* whose bitterness might be said to grow out of his discovery that his pseudofamily, Bryon and his mother, to whom he had been kidding himself in imagining he belonged, had never truly made him a part of their plans. A real family would make no fine "then" and "now" distinctions. As Johnny Cade said of pseudofamilies: "It ain't the same as having your own folks care about you. . . . It just ain't the same."

Along with these dreams, Tex shares with Ponyboy and Rusty-James the nightmares, the waking in a cold sweat in the middle of the night, the fears of an abandonment that has already taken place. Ponyboy can't remember his dreams, but Tex's are visual and desolate, a "big expanse of empty white space." There is an element almost of deliberate cruelty in the way all these kids have been left behind, like Rusty-James abandoned for three days alone in an empty house, and it is no wonder that their dreams are haunted by visions of loneliness and desolation.

The only answer to this loneliness is to feel that one finally belongs, somewhere, sometime. Without that sense of security, of belonging, the future will remain, as it seems at first for Tex, "a foggy pit [where he is] standing on the edge, trying to see bottom, knowing any minute something was going to shove me in." Unfortunately for Tex, in order to escape this foggy pit he makes what must have seemed to him (as at first it did to us) the obvious choice for belonging, for adoption: he pins his hopes on Pop, his father. Pop, alas, is worse than the wrong choice; what he knows threatens to send Tex far deeper into the foggy pit than he wants to go.

Tex's reaction to this new knowledge, to the completeness of his abandonment, is an interesting departure from what we might have expected from the earlier books. He doesn't rant and rave and get angry about it, as Ponyboy might have done. He doesn't blame the world, as Mark ultimately does. He doesn't go limp and numb, as do Rusty-James and Bryon. Instead he has a curiously calm reaction: he turns and runs from the school, but not wild and out of control, as might be anyone's first reaction. He runs "steadily, timing my breathing. . . . Almost like I knew where I was going. Almost like I had somewhere to go." His words suggest the entrance on stage of that dark character from *Rumble Fish,* Fate.

Prophecy and the Victory over Fate

> "Tell Rusty-James that life does go
> on, if you'll let it."
> —Cassandra, *Rumble Fish*

Rusty-James is not equipped to take Cassandra's advice (he calls her "a dingbat" instead), but for Tex, who has a healthy respect for prophecy in all its forms, it is the sort of thing he could hardly ignore. The influence of myth and prophecy, so prominent in *Rumble Fish,* reappears to play a major role in *Tex* as well. The scene with the carnival gypsy sets the tone: "Your far past:

You are a fourth-generation cowboy. Your near past: violence and sorrow. Your next year: change. My best advice: Don't change. Your future: There are people who go, people who stay. You will stay."

Jamie the rationalist is no believer (the gypsy predicts three marriages for her in the future, a fortune that doesn't please her, although it seems to us that the gypsy might have even missed a marriage or two), but Tex is. Tex—the antirationalist, the natural man in the Huck Finn American tradition—knows and expects that prophecy and myth will have an effect upon his life. Like the bad luck brought on by the rattlesnake skin in *Huckleberry Finn*, the gypsy's prophecy will stand—it becomes part of the "truth" that Tex is forced to live with. As Huck himself puts it: "There warn't anything to say. We both [he and Jim] knowed well enough it was some more work of the rattlesnake-skin; so what was the use to talk about it? It would only look like we was finding fault, and that would be bound to fetch more bad luck—and keep on fetching it, too, till we knowed enough to keep still."[9]

After the gypsy's prophecy, the nature of Tex's reality rearranges itself into "those who go and those who stay." Her reference to the generations of cowboys in his lineage comes back to haunt him. Johnny's use of the term "throwback . . . like when you breed a chestnut to a black and get an Albino colt like its great grandfather," comes to have a much more prophetic resonance as the book goes along, like a time bomb of fate, hiding in the genes. (The concept of "throwback" is salvaged from *That Was Then, This Is Now*. One of the challenges of *Tex* is to take this restrictive, deterministic concept and set it free.)

Tex discovers that there is a way to triumph over fate, and over truth, however harsh it may be. It involves an acceptance of the ground rules of fate—not as the end of a process but as a beginning. Fighting against the ground rules is pointless; you end up like Rusty-James, numb and sealed off from the world, or like Lem, who "looked just plain clumsy in [his city] kitchen." "There are people who go places and people who stay and Lem should have stayed."

No, the way to beat fate is to beat it at its own game, to be as resilient as Smoky the Cowhorse, and to recognize that "if you were where you wanted to be . . . you weren't stuck [at all]." When Mason says, at the end of the book, that he was sure that Tex would hate him, hate all of them when he found out the truth, he shows that he is unaware of something Tex has learned. What he has learned is the lesson the noble heroes of Greek tragedy and Greek mythology knew: it is perhaps impossible to avoid being the prisoner of fate, but by accepting its limitations and by working with dignity within those limitations, it is always possible to avoid being the victim of fate.

The hope for perfection in the world that sparked much of the idealism of *The Outsiders* has pretty much disappeared by the time of *Tex*. All the "perfect" parents are gone. The Motorcycle Boy, the "perfect knight," has no place in this world. Staying gold has come to mean, not the truculent "I'll never grow up" of Peter Pan, but the bitter acknowledgment of Bryon Douglas at the end of *That Was Then, This Is Now*: "I wish I was a kid again, when I had all the answers." Bryon is being ironic; staying gold now means being a fool.

Into this vale of imperfection comes Tex, who has the rare stubbornness of Will James's cowhorse, and the optimism of another, more famous literary character, also an illegitimate, Voltaire's Candide. Tex has Candide's practical wisdom and, as he discovers that there is no Garden of Eden made up for him on this earth, he determines instead that it will be necessary for him to cultivate a garden of his own.[10]

Candide and the Problem of Evil

—My dear girl, replied Candide,
when a man is in love, jealous, and
just whipped by the Inquisition, he is
no longer himself.
                      —Voltaire, *Candide,* 1759

We in the modern world no longer worry much about the Problem of Evil; no one suggests that this is "the best of possible worlds." Nevertheless, there is an analogous problem in the modern world and it is a particular problem of the books *That Was Then, This Is Now* and *Tex*. What causes people to change for the worse, to descend into violence? Why does hate suddenly rise up and overcome people for whom other choices, other outcomes could have been possible? This is an infection of nearly all the characters in *That Was Then, This Is Now,* from the black girl in the story-within-a-story to Bryon to, finally, Mark, his "brother." What explains the transformation of Mark from the "friendly lion" to the man "with the golden, hard, flat eyes of a jungle animal?"

This question is never adequately dealt with in *That Was Then, This Is Now.* It's all a mishmash of hatred and regret at the end, but the question of evil, and responsibility for it, is left unanswered. For the characters of *That Was Then, This Is Now,* the fact is that there probably is no answer. They have not cultivated the resources necessary to provide one.

In any event, Hinton will not leave those characters in the unresolved state of the book's ending. She will bring them back, to let them play out the string and—most important—to explore the contrast between Mark, the Peter Pan of *That Was Then, This Is Now,* and Tex, his "little brother." This contrast becomes obvious when they first meet, when Tex pulls to the side of the road and picks up Mark the hitchhiker.

The Return of Mark the Lion

It begins when we notice that Tex has Mark's hair and coloring, "a light bright gold-brown, the same color as my eyes." We remember Mark's "gold hair and strange gold eyes" and how his eyes give his true lineage away ("Nobody on my side of the family has eyes that color"), just as Tex's eyes betray him each day of his life, as he strives, in what he does not yet know is a hopeless effort, to win Pop's affection.

It continues with the odd similarity of the rodeo riders who are described as the true biological fathers of each of them. Mark describes his heroically: "My real father was a cowboy, here for the rodeo. The old lady said he had gold hair and gold eyes just like mine and that he won all kinds of prizes at the rodeo."

Tex, on the other hand, has only Pop's description of his true father, a description that is, not unexpectedly, something less than heroic: "I know who your daddy was. . . . He was a rodeo rider; I haven't seen him on the circuit so somebody's husband or daddy probably shot him a long time ago. Yeller-eyed tomcat, he was hanging around her, even before." How many golden-eyed, philandering cowboys could that rodeo circuit have produced?

In any case, Tex and Mark meet (Mark has dyed his lion gold hair "a muddy brown color") and Tex knows right away that this hitchhiker is not a stranger, from out of town, but is "from around here. . . . He reminded me of somebody, but I couldn't think who." We find out "who" at the end of the chapter.

Mark has just come from Tulsa, where he had gone first after his escape from prison, because he thought he "had business to take care of," the "business" being his long-cherished revenge on Bryon Douglas, a violence that was suggested ("I think if he could have, Mark would have killed me") at the end of *That Was Then, This Is Now*.

Ironically, as Bryon himself had discovered in that earlier book, Mark finds that "the big revenge trip" he had planned was a hollow event, "him lying there looking up at me, and he says, 'Get it over with,' and it was like all the air out of a balloon. All these years . . . and then I just didn't feel like finishing it. . . . I was just too plain bored." (Which doesn't mean that he is too bored to shoot Bryon, only that he is too bored to bother finishing him off.)

Mark also realizes that by choosing the revenge trip he is at the same time most likely sealing his fate. "And to think I could have been planning something constructive all this time, like the quickest way out of the country." He's doomed and he knows it, but he's been beyond caring about that for much too long.

Tex does what he has to do. He runs the truck off the road to save Mason and himself. The hitchhiker tries to drag Mason out with him, as a hostage, but Tex holds on. At last "the hitchhiker let go and gave me a funny little cat grin before he disappeared back of the truck." There's a moment of communication there (the "funny little cat grin" is reminiscent of an earlier Mark, one still capable of being saved); there's a moment of brief understanding, perhaps. Later, when Tex goes to look at him, "His sunglasses had fallen off but nobody had shut his eyes yet. He was staring up at the sky he couldn't see anymore with a bitter expression in his strange-colored eyes," and we know that, for Mark, the long struggle with a world in which he could not, would not, fit, is over.

Tex takes responsibility for Mark's death (something we know neither Mark nor Bryon would have done) and at the end of the chapter there is this odd conversation between Mason and Tex:

> "Mace, something really bad must have happened to that guy. I mean, he was really a terrible person."
>
> Mason just nodded. It was a little bit later that he surprised me by saying, "You don't think you could ever turn out like that?"
>
> I thought a little bit before I answered—it sure was a time for thinking about things.
>
> "Well, I don't think so. But then nothing really bad has ever happened to me."
>
> "That's true," Mason said carefully. It was then I knew who it was that guy had reminded me of.
>
> It was me.

In case this identification needs strengthening, we may recall the earlier conversation, in *That Was Then, This Is Now*, between Bryon and Mark, in which Bryon complains,

> "Pow! Care about somebody, give a damn for another person, and you get blasted. How come it's like that?"
>
> "You got me, Bryon. I never thought about it. I guess 'cause nothin' bad has ever happened to me."

Out of such similar, innocent, hopeful pasts they arrived at such disparate fates. Where Voltaire's people asked why God permitted such bitterness and violence, we in this secular time are reduced to asking the same question of ourselves: where did we go wrong?

The easy answer—and consequently the one most often heard—is that it's society's fault. We already know what Ponyboy thinks of this "pity-the-victims-of-environment junk." Blaming society provides no relief to those who are suffering; it merely shifts responsibility from individuals to an imaginary, impersonal structure not much different from Pangloss's "best of possible worlds." The answer, if there is one, must lie elsewhere, and for Hinton characters the logical place to look is the same place where Ponyboy's paradise is to be found: inside themselves. "Something bad" seems to have happened to all of them, but only Tex has the inner resources, like Candide, to turn that misfortune not into further evil but into hopefulness. As Bryon Douglas says in the earlier book, the cycle of revenge has to stop somewhere ("It's stupid and I'm sick of it and it keeps going in circles"), but Bryon can't stop it; he's locked into it just as he's locked into himself. Only Tex can stop it and, amazingly enough, he does.

What Tex has that the other characters lack is that rare generosity of his, that ability to break out of the prison of himself and to feel a sympathy for others. Rusty-James had some of this talent, too, but he invested it all in the Motorcycle Boy and when he lost the Motorcycle Boy he lost everything. Tex doesn't have any preferred investments; he seems to invest in everybody. As a result, his stock never falls, he's always got someone to hope for, and something to look forward to. It's never anything major, but that's the point, that's where his "contentment" comes from. He knows, as Huck Finn put it, how "to keep still," to concentrate on doing the work that needs to be done, on cultivating the garden.

The lesson of *Candide,* and of *Tex,* is that, after all the talking and philosophizing, life requires work. It is not—nor should it ever be mistaken for—a gift that comes fully valued and ready to be cashed in. There's nothing hereditary about success in life; it's no one's birthright, and it's just as available to Tulsa orphans as to anyone else, if they are willing to work at it. "Let's work without speculating," says one of the characters at the end of *Candide*. Let's quit talking and get to work. It is significant that, as the novel ends, Tex's first real job, at the Kencaide Quarter Horse farm, begins.

Hinton has said, "It seems to me the underlying message is that you're going to take the responsibility for your own actions ultimately. I don't care what excuses or explanations you've got."[11] It is this knowledge, finally, that separates Tex from his half-brother Mark.

Cathy, another character from *That Was Then, This Is Now* (whom we last saw in that book dazed by Bryon's rejection, but on the arm of Ponyboy Curtis) also appears in *Tex*. She is Miss Carlson, Tex's English teacher. When he learns she has gone to Mark's funeral, Tex asks her about it, asks if he were a relative. Cathy says no, "Not even a friend, really." She goes on to talk about the past, and the meaning of the past is no more clear to her now than it had been then. "I can't explain to you what Mark was to me, exactly. I knew him a long time ago." Tex, with all his generosity and sympathy showing, "feeling like I do when I bump into things," says he's sorry.

Cathy tells him not to be. She may not understand the past but, like Tex, she has learned a few lessons on how to proceed with the future. " 'I'm sad about what happened, but not surprised.' She glanced down into her grade book. 'Now what ever happened to that other book report?' "

We must get to work. We must cultivate our garden.

Appendix

Film Adaptations

Tex

Cast:
 Tex McCormick—Matt Dillon
 Mason McCormick—Jim Metzler
 Jamie Collins—Meg Tilly
 Pop McCormick—Bill McKinney
 Cole Collins—Ben Johnson
 Johnny Collins—Emilio Estevez
 Lem Peters—Phil Brock
 Hitchhiker—Zeljko Ivanek

Director—Tim Hunter
Producer—Tim Zinnemann
Screenplay—Charlie Haas and Tim Hunter
Photography—Ric Waite

A Walt Disney release
Opened September 1982

 Hinton took some time before allowing Disney to film *Tex*, the first of her books to be adapted for the movies. She says that her biggest fear was that they would film something like "Tex and the Seven Dwarfs," a prospect that did not please her. Horror stories about what happens to books on their way to the screen abound, but in this case, and in the case of her other three books as well, Hinton was more fortunate than most.

 Tim Hunter seems to have taken extraordinary care with the translation to the screen. The screen version of *Tex* is faithful to the book in nearly every way possible. Even where it departs from the book it never goes out of character. A good example is Tex's interception and hiding of Mason's Indiana University admissions application (and his later change of heart, filling it out, with Jamie, and sending it). Nothing like this happens in the book but, as Hinton herself admits, it's just the sort of thing Tex would do.

Disney came to Tulsa to shoot the movie (as did most of the later film companies) and Tim Hunter kept Hinton busy during the course of the production. She helped him select locations for the various scenes, and coached some of the actors on their parts. She also introduced Matt Dillon to her horse, Toyota, and taught him to ride. Tim Hunter talked Hinton into playing a small part in the film (she's the typing teacher who's the victim of Tex's prank with the caps) and Hunter remains a good friend to this day.

All in all, the film *Tex* was warmly received, and there are some who contend that it was the vehicle that made Matt Dillon a star. Hinton has said that it is probably her favorite of the films, and it has held up well over the years. With good performances from Dillon, Metzler, and Tilley (not to mention Toyota), it possesses some of the same "unexpected contentment" the book had, no small achievement in the realm of tradition overkill that is Hollywood.

The Outsiders

Cast:
Dallas Winston—Matt Dillon
Johnny Cade—Ralph Macchio
Ponyboy Curtis—C. Thomas Howell
Darrel Curtis—Patrick Swayze
Sodapop Curtis—Rob Lowe
Two-Bit Mathews—Emilio Estevez
Steve Randle—Tom Cruise
Cherry Valance—Diane Lane
Bob Sheldon—Leif Garrett

Director—Francis Ford Coppola
Producer—Fred Roos and Gray Frederickson
Screenplay—Kathleen Knutsen Rowell
Music—Carmine Coppola

A Warner Brothers release
Opened March 1983

The dedication at the end of the film reads: "The film *The Outsiders* is dedicated to the people who first suggested that it be made—librarian Jo Ellen Misakian and the students of The Lone Star School in Fresno,

California." This must be a first, when a group of seventh and eight graders can cause Hollywood to gear up for a $10 million movie. The result, unfortunately, is not the best of the Hinton screen adaptations.

The problems began with Rowell's screenplay, which was then written and rewritten by other hands (including Coppola's, with a little help from Hinton), until it may have been written out of existence. The cinematography is extremely flashy; multicolored sunsets seem to dominate the film and in some ways, perhaps, it is Coppola's penchant for taking chances, for going after the big effect, that is responsible for the disjointed, overblown impression the film finally leaves with us. Some of the critics compared it to opera in its effect, and this is not at all a compliment. Coppola tried to expand the story of *The Outsiders* into something like myth, into a statement about youth and America, and unfortunately the continuity of the story itself got lost somewhere (probably on the cutting room floor). The movie can still be a great experience, particularly for those who are thoroughly familiar with the book, but on its own, as a film, it is not as successfully as *Tex*.

Hinton was probably more involved with the making of *The Outsiders* than she was with *Tex*. In fact she was a paid consultant of sorts and when occasionally she was not present on the set as expected, Coppola let her know about it. In general, her experience with the film was extremely valuable and satisfying; she became especially close to the film's young cast. Once again she appears on screen, cast as a nurse who is hassled by Dallas (Matt Dillon), which was a part she says she felt comfortable with, since it mimicked the kind of kidding that went on all the time on the set.

The movie was a commercial success (it grossed $5 million over the first weekend of its release) but it remains a disappointment compared to what it might have been.

Rumble Fish

Cast:

> Rusty-James—Matt Dillon
> Motorcycle Boy—Mickey Rourke
> Patty—Diane Lane
> Father—Dennis Hopper
> Cassandra—Diana Scarwid
> Steve—Vincent Spano
> Smokey—Nicolas Cage
> B. J.—Christopher Penn
> Benny—Tom Waits

Director—Francis Coppola

Producer—Fred Roos and Doug Claybourne
Photography—Stephen H. Burum
Screenplay—S. E. Hinton and Francis Ford Coppola
Music—Stewart Copeland

A Universal Pictures release
Opened October 1983

Hinton and Coppola wrote the screenplay for *Rumble Fish* during the filming of *The Outsiders*. They worked at it on Sundays, the one day off from shooting during the earlier film. The translation from book to film is, as with *Tex,* quite accurate. Hinton contributed her dialogue and Coppola attempted to take the moody, dark atmosphere of the book and relate it in cinematic terms. There is some disagreement as to whether the film is successful. For those who don't think so, the charges are much the same as with *The Outsiders,* that it is overblown, operatic, pretentious. For those who do, the film is an experience much like the book: eerie, allusive, attentive to the mythical element of life. The two sides will never agree but that is fairly typical of the reception accorded the book as well.

Matt Dillon appears again, as Rusty-James, and manages to expand the swaggering tough guy roles he had been cast in to include the vulnerability and hero worship that makes Rusty-James such a singular character. Mickey Rourke brings a touch of humanity even to the Motorcycle Boy, something the book didn't do. The role of Patty is expanded somewhat for Diane Lane, and she does a good job with it. Patty is much more the injured party in the movie than she is in the book. The other actors are fine, as well. Hinton appears in a bit part, playing a streetwalker in the carnival-like city scene, but that's not her voice we hear; the voice was overdubbed, "looped," back in Hollywood.

The film is shot in black and white, an allusion to the color blindness of the Motorcycle Boy but also a good representation of the mood of the story. The concerns of the story are closer to the black and white concerns of classics like Bergman's *Seventh Seal*—characters playing chess with Death and the like—than they are with the typical Hollywood Technicolor extravaganza. Only the fish are in color, tinted red and blue, swimming around over the black and white screen like creatures from another dimension. Coppola is, as usual, not afraid to put himself on the line, to risk ridicule even, in order to keep faith with the vision. As a result we have a movie that is the cinematic equivalent of the book, a fable unconstrained by space and time, more like a haunting piece of music (helped immeasurably by Stewart Copeland's score) than a movie narrative. It's one of the few films I would want to have on hand in my home video library.

That Was Then, This Is Now

Cast:
  Mark Jennings—Emilio Estevez
  Bryon Douglas—Craig Sheffer
  Cathy Carlson—Kim Delaney
  M&M—Frank Howard
  Mrs. Douglas—Barbara Babcock
  Charlie—Morgan Freeman

Director—Christopher Cain
Producer—Gary R. Lindberg and John M. Ondov
Screenplay—Emilio Estevez
Photography—Juan Ruiz Anchia

A Paramount Pictures release
Opened November 1985

That Was Then, This Is Now was the only film adaptation in which Hinton was not involved. Emilio Estevez, a veteran of Hinton films, having appeared in both *Tex* and *The Outsiders*, wrote the screenplay and starred as Mark Jennings. It is interesting to note that *That Was Then, This Is Now* is the only film in which significant changes were made in the story line inherited from the book. First of all, unlike the other three books, *That Was Then, This Is Now* seems much more located in a certain time, the late sixties, with its communes and long hair and peace medals. Most of this is eliminated in the film, which makes it less time-dependent, although it also makes M&M's role a little ambivalent. In the book he's clearly a proto-hippie, while in the movie he's just vulnerable and strange.

More important, many of the "hard choices" of the book are softened for the movies. The Mark Jennings of the movie does indeed sell M&M the drug that does him in, which makes Bryon's decision to betray him a little more palatable, and the hatred with which the book ends is turned into a scene of something like nostalgia in the movie. Because of this, the movie is much more conventional and easier to deal with than the book. Hollywood moved in to smooth out the rough spots. This doesn't make it a bad film; it just makes *Rumble Fish* look that much more courageous.

Notes and References

1. Who Is This S. E. Hinton . . . ?

1. The quotations attributed to Hinton in this chapter, and throughout the book, are primarily from three sources: a talk she gave at the Boston Public Library on 20 September 1980; an interview with Linda Plemons, "Author Laureate of Adolescent Fiction," in the *University of Tulsa Annual, 1983–84;* and personal conversations with the author. Whenever possible I have tried to use documented sources for the quotations, rather than memory of conversations.

2. *Author Biographies Master Index,* 2d ed. (Detroit: Gale, 1984), 669.

3. Quoted by Yvonne Litchfield, "Her Book to be Published Soon, But Tulsa Teen-Ager Keeps Cool," *Tulsa Daily World,* 7 April 1967, 20.

4. Autobiographical Sketch of Susan Eloise Hinton Inhofe, *Fourth Book of Junior Authors and Illustrators* (New York: Wilson, 1978), 176.

5. Neal R. Peirce, *The Great Plains States of America* (New York: Norton, 1973), 272.

6. Ibid., 275.

7. Lou Willett Stanek, "Real People, Real Books: About YA Readers," *Top of the News,* June 1975, 417.

8. Apparently it is now the opposite. In the Plemons interview, Hinton says, "E. L. Doctorow told me once as soon as he used his initials everybody thought he was a woman."

9. Quoted by Ellis Widner in an article in *Tulsa World,* 20 March 1981, shortly after the successful movie option of *Tex.*

10. Zena Sutherland, "The Teen-Ager Speaks," *Saturday Review,* 27 January 1968, 34.

11. From Litchfield, "Her Book," 20.

2. The Outsiders

1. *Kirkus Reviews.* 15 April 1967, 506–7 (J–178–79).

2. New York Times Book Review, 7 May 1967, pt. 2, 10–12.

3. *Horn Book Magazine,* August 1967, 475.

4. *Saturday Review,* 13 May 1967, 59.

5. *Library Journal,* 15 May 1967, 2028–29.

6. Ibid., 2029.

7. S. E. Hinton, "Teen-agers Are for Real," *New York Times Book Review,* 27 August 1967, 26–29.

8. Quoted in Sutherland, "Teen-ager," 34.

9. Talk at the Boston Public Library, 20 September 1980.

10. Richard Peck, "In the Country of Teenage Fiction," *American Libraries,* April 1973, 204.

11. From J. M. Barrie's *Peter and Wendy,* an early novelization of the *Peter Pan* play, quoted in Andrew Birkin, *J. M. Barrie and the Lost Boys* (New York: Clarkson Potter, 1979), 163. This is a scene where Peter comes back to find Wendy grown up, a married woman with a daughter of her own. She can no longer fly away with him. Her "young and innocent" daughter, however, who awakens to find Peter crying, just as her mother had found him twenty years earlier ("Boy, why are you crying?"), can and does.

12. Quoted in Birkin, *J. M. Barrie,* 164.

3. That Was Then, This Is Now

1. Quoted in Plemons interview, 66.

2. Litchfield, "Her Book," 20.

3. Plemons interview, 65.

4. Litchfield, "Her Book," 20.

5. Quoted in Jheri Fleet, "Of Success for the Tulsa Writer," *OK Magazine,* 6 December 1981, 9.

6. Autobiographical Sketch, *Fourth Book,* 177.

7. Boston Public Library talk.

8. *Library Journal,* 15 June 1971, 2138.

9. *Booklist,* 15 July 1971, 951.

10. *Publisher's Weekly,* 31 May 1971, 135.

11. *Horn Book Magazine,* August 1971, 389.

12. *Saturday Review,* 19 June 1971, 27.

13. Ibid.

14. Zena Sutherland, *The Best in Children's Books* (Chicago: University of Chicago Press, 1973), 182.

15. All the Cart quotations are from the *New York Times Book Review,* 8 August 1971, 8.

16. Autobiographical Sketch, *Fourth Book,* 177.

4. Rumble Fish

1. Plemons interview, 64.
2. *Publisher's Weekly,* 28 July 1975, 122.
3. *Kirkus Reviews,* 15 October 1975, 1193.
4. *Horn Book Magazine,* December 1975, 601.
5. *Growing Point,* May 1976, 2894.
6. *The Outsiders,* (New York: Viking, 60).
7. P. M. Matarasso, trans., *The Quest of the Holy Grail,* (London: Penguin Books, 1969), 279.
8. Ibid., 17.
9. Flannery O'Connor, *The Complete Stories* (New York: Farrar, Straus & Giroux, 1971), 133.
10. *New York Times Book Review,* 14 December 1975, 8.

5. Tex

1. Patricia J. Campbell, "The Young Adult Perplex," *Wilson Library Bulletin,* October 1979, 122.
2. Paxton Davis's review in the *New York Times Book Review,* 16 December 1979, 23, while having qualities of a serious review, treating the book as a novel rather than a sociological tract, cannot, alas, refrain from schoolmarmish disapprobation: "Even by the standards of today's fiction, S. E. Hinton's vision of contemporary teen-age life is riper than warrants belief."
David Rees in *Times Literary Supplement,* 28 March 1980, 356, takes the superficial view that "the dust jacket tells all: our blond-haired hero is shown looking like an updated surly James Dean, motorbike protruding between his legs, with the title Tex—hard, macho name—in big red letters underneath."
3. *School Library Journal,* November 1979, 88.
4. *Growing Point,* May 1980, 3686.
5. This, and the shorter quotes immediately following, are from the Plemons interview.
6. Ibid.
7. In the Plemons interview Hinton says, "I can see great similarities between at least my way of writing, and acting. I really have to become that narrator, but at least I don't have to do it with people staring at me" (65).
8. Boston Public Library talk.
9. Mark Twain, *The Adventures of Huckleberry Finn* (New York: Harper, 1884), 134.
10. A recent example of *Candide's* pervasive influence occurs in

Philip Hamburger, "Searching for Gregorian" (a profile of Vartan Gregorian, president of the New York Public Library,) *New Yorker,* 14 April 1986, 61, which contains the following observation: "The New York *Times Book Review* once asked me what character in literature I would most like to be. I instantly replied Candide. His deep concern for humanity. His critical rationalism. His healthy skepticism. His realistic optimism. His knowledge that with a frank acceptance of man's fate life can be made endurable. Candide calls for positive action, for faith in man's eventual ability to improve the human condition. One must cultivate one's own garden."

11. Patricia J. Campbell, "The Young Adult Perplex," *Wilson Library Bulletin,* September 1985, 62.

Selected Bibliography

Primary Sources

1. Novels

The Outsiders. New York: Viking Press, 1967. Reprint. New York: Dell, 1980.
Rumble Fish. New York: Delacorte Press, 1975. Reprint. New York: Dell, 1976.
Tex. New York: Delacorte Press, 1979. Reprint. New York: Dell, 1982.
That Was Then, This Is Now. New York, Viking Press, 1971. Reprint. New York: Dell, 1980.

2. Other

"Rumble Fish" (short story). *Nimrod*, Special Literary Supplement to the *University of Tulsa Alumni Magazine*, October 1968, 4.
"Teen-Agers Are for Real" (article). *New York Times Book Review*, 27 August 1967, 26.

Secondary Sources

1. Books, Monographs, etc.

Barrie, J. M. *Peter Pan, or The Boy Who Would Not Grow Up*. New York: Scribner's, 1928.
Birkin, Andrew. *J. M. Barrie and the Lost Boys*. New York: Clarkson Potter, 1979.
James, Will. *Smoky the Cowhorse*. New York: Scribner's, 1926.

Lenz, Millicent, and Mahood, Ramona, eds. *Young Adult Literature.* Chicago: American Library Association, 1980.

Stanek, Lou Willett. *A Teacher's Guide to the Paperback Editions of the Novels of S. E. Hinton.* New York: Dell, 1975, 1980.

Sutherland, Zena. *The Best in Children's Books.* Chicago: University of Chicago Press, 1973.

Varlejs, Jana, ed. *Young Adult Literature in the Seventies.* Metuchen, N. J.: Scarecrow, 1978.

2. Articles

Farber, Stephen. "Directors Join the S. E. Hinton Fan Club." *New York Times,* 20 March 1983, p. 2, 19.

Peck, Richard. "In the Country of Teenage Fiction." *American Libraries,* April 1973, 204.

Robin, Lisa. "S. E. Hinton Knows How to Write for the Young and the Restless." *Media and Methods,* May-June 1982, 28.

Stanek, Lou Willett. "Real People, Real Books: About YA Readers." *Top of the News,* June 1975, 417.

Sutherland, Zena. "The Teen-Ager Speaks." *Saturday Review,* 27 January 1968, 94.

3. Interviews, Speeches

Campbell, Patricia J. "The Young Adult Perplex" *Wilson Library Bulletin,* September 1985, 62.

Hinton, S. E. Talk at the Boston Public Library 20 September 1980. Audio recording.

Plemons, Linda. "Author Laureate of Adolescent Fiction." *University of Tulsa Annual, 1983–84,* 62.

4. Book Reviews (selected)

The Outsiders
Booklist 1 October 1967, 176.

Fleming, Thomas. *New York Times Book Review,* 7 May 1967, pt.2, 10.

Gerhardt, Lillian. *Library Journal,* 15 May 1967, 2028.

Hentoff, Nat. *Atlantic Monthly,* December 1967, 136.

Kirkus Reviews, 15 April 1967, 506 (J–178).

Manthorne, Jane. *Horn Book Magazine,* August 1967, 475.

Sutherland, Zena. *Saturday Review,* 13 May 1967, 59.

That Was Then, This Is Now
Andrews, Sheryl B. *Horn Book Magazine,* August 1971, 388.
Anson, Brooke. *Library Journal,* 15 June 1971, 2138.
Booklist, 15 July 1971, 951.
Cart, Michael. *New York Times Book Review,* 8 August 1971, 8.
Publisher's Weekly, 31 May 1971, 135.
Sutherland, Zena. *Saturday Review,* 19 June 1971, 27.

Rumble Fish
Abramson, Jane. *School Library Journal,* October 1975, 106.
Amis, Martin. *New Statesman,* 21 March 1976, 690.
Berkvist, Robert. *New York Times Book Review,* 14 December 1975, 8.
Booklist, 1 September 1975, 41.
Fisher, Margery. *Growing Point,* May 1976, 2894.
Kirkus Reviews, 15 October 1975, 1193.
Publisher's Weekly, 28 July 1975, 122.
Silvey, Anita. *Horn Book Magazine,* December 1975, 601.

Tex
Campbell, Patricia J. *Wilson Library Bulletin,* October 1979, 122.
Davis, Paxton. *New York Times Book Review,* 16 December 1979, 23.
Fisher, Margery. *Growing Point,* May 1980, 3686.
Kaye, Marilyn. *School Library Journal,* November 1979, 88.
Rees, David. *Times Literary Supplement,* 28 March 1980, 356.
Wilms, Denise M. *Booklist,* 15 October 353.

Index

About the Author

Jay Daly is the author of the young adult novel *Walls* (Harper & Row, 1980; reprint ed., Dell, 1981) as well as a number of short stories and articles. He was a teaching fellow in the Writing Program at Boston University during 1980–81, and his fiction won awards from the Massachusetts Artists Foundation in 1985 and 1986. He lives with his daughter Eowyn in Brookline, Massachusetts.